P9-BJJ-534

INSTRUCTOR'S MANUAL WITH VIDEO GUIDE
James V. Dupree

BEHAVIOR IN ORGANIZATIONS

Sixth Edition

Jerald Greenberg
Robert A. Baron

INSTRUCTOR'S MANUAL
WITH VIDEO GUIDE

BEHAVIOR IN ORGANIZATIONS

Sixth Edition

INSTRUCTOR'S MANUAL WITH VIDEO GUIDE

James V. Dupree

Grove City College

BEHAVIOR IN ORGANIZATIONS

Sixth Edition

Jerald Greenberg
Robert A. Baron

Prentice Hall, Upper Saddle River, New Jersey 07458

Project Editor: *Evyan Jengo*
Acquisitions Editor: *Natalie Anderson*
Editorial Assistant : *Chrissy Statuto*
Manufacturing Buyer: *Arnold Vila*

 © 1997 by Prentice Hall, Inc.
A Simon & Schuster Company
Upper Saddle River, NJ 07458

Printed in the United States of America

10 9 8 7 6 5 4 3 2

ISBN 0-13-568213-4

Prentice-Hall International (UK) Limited, *London*
Prentice-Hall of Australia Pty. Limited, *Sydney*
Prentice-Hall Canada Inc., *Toronto*
Prentice-Hall Hispanoamericana, S.A., *Mexico*
Prentice-Hall of India Private Limited, *New Delhi*
Prentice-Hall of Japan, Inc., *Tokyo*
Simon & Schuster Asia Pte. Ltd., *Singapore*
Editora Prentice-Hall do Brasil, Ltda., *Rio de Janiero*

Table of Contents

Part 1 - Organizational Behavior: An Introduction

Chapter 1 The Nature and Study of Organizations 1

Chapter 2 Work in the Twenty-First Century:
  The Changing World of People and Organizations 12

Part 2 - Basic Human Processes

Chapter 3 Perception and Learning:
  Understanding and Adapting to the Work Environment 26

Chapter 4 Individual Differences:
  Personality and Abilities 38

Part 3 - The Individual in the Organization

Chapter 5 Motivation in Organizations 48

Chapter 6 Work-Related Attitudes:
  Feelings About Jobs, Organizations, and People 57

Chapter 7 Career Development and Work Stress 67

Part 4 - Group Processes

Chapter 8 Group Dynamics and Teamwork 79

Chapter 9 Interpersonal Communication in Organizations 91

Chapter 10 Decision Making in Organizations 104

Chapter 11 Helping, Cooperation, And Conflict in Organizations 117

Part 5 - Influencing Others

Chapter 12 Influence, Power, and Politics in Organizations 128

Chapter 13 Leadership:
  Its Nature and Impact on Organizations 136

Chapter 14 The Work Environment:
  Culture and Technology 147

Part 6 - Organizational Processes

Chapter 15 Organizational Structure and Design 157

Chapter 16 Organizational Change and Development 169

Video Cases

Part I   When Employees Become Owners
             The Changing Face of Labor **180**

Part II   Working Fathers Balance Careers and Family
             The Joys and Risks of the "Daddy Track" **181**

Part III Looking for More Cal Ripkens
             The Streak: Cal Ripken, Jr. **182**

Part IV   Do Communication Rituals Hold Back Women in the Workplace?
             He Says She Says—Women's Business Style is a Handicap **183**

Part V   Ben & Jerry's: A New Leader to Manage Growth
             Sharing Sweet Success **184**

Part VI   Telecommuting
             Telecommuting **185**

Video Guides

Southwest Airlines
Southwest Airlines **186**

Hiring Practices at Japanese-Owned Companies
No Room at the Top **187**

Workplace Violence
Back with a Vengeance **188**

Controversy Over Sensitivity Training by the FAA
When the Tables are Turned **189**

Learning Objectives

After reading this chapter you, should be able to:

1. Describe the major focus of the fields of *organizational behavior*, including the three basic units of analysis used.
2. Characterize the major characteristics of the field of organizational behavior today.
3. Explain how the study of organizational behavior relies upon a *contingency approach*.
4. Trace the historical developments and schools of thought leading up to the field of organizational behavior today.
5. Explain the importance of the *scientific method* in learning about behavior in organizations.
6. Describe the role of theory in the pursuit of knowledge about organizational behavior.
7. Characterize the major approaches to conducting research in the field of organizational behavior and compare the relative advantages and disadvantages of each.

Chapter Contents   Page

Introduction   2
I. Organizational Behavior: A Working Definition   4
    A. OB applies the Scientific Method to Practical Managerial Problems   4
    B. OB Focuses on Three Levels of Analysis: Individuals, Groups, and Organizations   5

II. Organizational Behavior Today: Characteristics of the Field   5
    A. OB Seeks to Improve People's Quality of Life at Work   6
    B. OB Recognizes the Dynamic Nature of Organizations   7
    C. OB Assumes There is No "One Best" Approach   8
    D. OB Confronts the Challenges Created by the Changing Nature of Work   10

III. Organizational Behavior: A Capsule History of the Field   11
    A. Scientific Management: The Roots of Organizational Behavior   11
    B. The Human Relations Movement: Elton Mayo and the Hawthorne Studies   12
    C. Classical Organization Theory   14
    D. Organizational Behavior in the Modern Era   16

IV. Theory and Research: Tools for Learning About Behavior in Organizations   17
    A. Isn't It All Just Common Sense?   17
    B. Theory: An Indispensable Guide to Organizational Research   18
    C. Survey Research: The Correlational Method   20
    D. Experimental Research: The Logic of Cause and Effect   23
    E. Qualitative Research: Naturalistic Observation and the Case Method   27
Summary and Review   29
Questions for Discussion   29
Case in Point   30
Skills Portfolios   30
    Experiencing Organizational Behavior   30
    Working in Groups   31

Chapter Outline

<u>Instructor's Notes</u>

<u>Case Preview</u> Discussion of CEO Herb Kelleher's management of Southwest Airlines and his cheerleading style.

<u>Introduction</u>
1. There is nothing magical about Herb Kelleher's style or success; he's simply realized that people are the key to organizational success. Organizational Behavior (OB) scientists and practitioners use behavioral sciences, such as psychology and sociology, to study and solve organizational problems.
2. This chapter will cover:
   a. Background information needed to understand the scope of OB and its value.
   b. It will introduce the student to:
      - its characteristics.
      - its history.
      - the tools it uses.
   c. The chapter begins with formal definitions and descriptions of OB.
      - Organizational behavior (OB) - the field specializing in the study of human behavior in organizations.
      - Behavioral sciences - psychology and sociology, tools within OB to study and solve problems in organizations.
   d. See Figure 1-1, cartoon.

I. <u>Organizational Behavior: A Working Definition</u>
   Definition - <u>Organizational behavior</u> is the field that seeks knowledge of behavior in organizational settings by systematically studying individual, group, and organizational processes.
   A. **OB Applies the Scientific Method to Practical Managerial Problems**
      1. OB is not as advanced as some fields of science like physics and chemistry because of its relative youth.
      2. It is important to learn about behavior in organizational settings for various reasons.
         - Human behavior is what makes people 'tick.'
         - It is the application of scientific studies.
         - It will help to improve the functioning of organizations.
         - It helps to answer important questions, such as:
            - How can goal setting enhance performance?
            - How may jobs be designed to improve feelings of satisfaction?
            - When do individuals make better decisions than groups?
            - Etc.

3. OB specialists not only apply their knowledge, they conduct studies to help solve specific problems.
   - These studies rely on the use of the scientific method as it is the central defining characteristic of modern organizational behavior.

B. **OB focuses on Three Levels of Analysis: Individuals, Groups, and Organizations**
   1. OB specialists look at behavior on three levels because individuals work in groups within an organizational setting.
   2. See Figure 1-2 for the three levels of analysis.

II. Organizational Behavior Today: Characteristics of the Field
   A. **OB Seeks to Improve People's Quality of Life at Work**
      1. The growth of the railroads and the demand for manufactured goods led many people from agriculture to manufacturing work. But they discovered a brutal work environment.
      2. Managers' traditional, negative view of employees was called Theory X by McGregor. They assumed people:
         - were lazy.
         - dislike work.
         - need direction.
         - must be geared to perform with a carrot or stick.
      3. Today's management view of employees is more optimistic. While some hold to the old Theory X view, many are recognizing employees for their efforts and seek to create positive working conditions.
      4. McGregor called this modern, optimistic view of employees Theory Y. It is assumed that people:
         - are not inherently lazy.
         - need to work.
         - seek responsibility and are worthy of trust.
      5. Theory Y predominates among those interested in organizational behavior.
      6. See Figure 1-4. A Summary of Theory X versus Theory Y.

   B. **OB Recognizes the Dynamic Nature of Organizations**
      1. OB pays attention to both behavior and the organizations within which the behavior takes place.
      2. **Definition** - Organization - is a structured social system consisting of groups of individuals working together to meet some agreed-upon objectives.
      3. Organizations are viewed as open systems, that is, self-sustaining systems that use energy to transform resources from the environment into some form of output.
         - See Figure 1-5. Models an organization as an open system.

C. OB Assumes There is No "One Best" Approach

1. Everyone wants to know what the best way to motivate is, to lead. There is no one best way to motivate people or to lead.
2. OB emphasizes a contingency approach--a recognition that behavior is the result of a complex of interacting forces and must be dealt with accordingly.
   - See Figure 1-6. This figure shows the three key elements that go into organizational behavior.
3. OB specialists agree that the best motivation and the best leadership style is contingent upon the circumstances of the behavior.
4. Simple cookbook answers are popular but not effective.

D. OB Confronts the Challenges Created by the Changing Nature of Work

1. The changing demographics of the workforce make the work of OB even more important.
   - There are more women working who are better trained and educated.
   - The relative proportion of African Americans, Asian Americans, and Hispanic Americans has increased while the number of native white Americans has declined.
   - See Figure 1-7. Diversity an Important Trend in the Workplace.
2. The economy has shifted from the U.S. being the dominate power to a global economy.
3. Not only has the workforce and the economy changed, the very nature of work has changed as well. The increased use of automation and sophisticated computer technology has raised new issues and challenges for OB.

III. <u>Organizational Behavior: A Capsule History of the Field</u>

A. Scientific Management: The Roots of Organizational Behavior

1. The earliest work came from efficiency experts seeking to improve worker productivity.
2. Frederick W. Taylor, who worked primarily in steel mills, developed the scientific method.
   - The objective of management is "to secure the maximum prosperity for the employer, coupled with the maximum prosperity of each employee."
3. Taylor's scientific management focused on employees as individuals.
   - Careful selection and training.
   - Increasing wages to motivate workers.
4. Frank and Lillian Gilbreth built on Taylor's ideas and

developed time-and-motion studies which classified and
streamlined work.

B. **The Human Relations Movement: Elton Mayo and the
Hawthorne Studies**
1. Scientific management made people feel like cogs in a
machine.
2. A new emphasis respecting the individual emerged and at
its forefront was Elton Mayo.
3. Human relations rejected the economic perspective of work
and focused on social factors.
4. The Hawthorne studies began in 1927 at Western Electric's
Hawthorne Works near Chicago.
  * Starting with scientific management, they tried to
discover ways to improve employee performance.
  * Puzzling results caused them to call in Elton Mayo to
repeat the studies.
  * Mayo discovered the concept of social systems and
argued that social factors, not physical factors, are
most important in improving productivity.
5. While the studies weren't perfect, they opened the door to
considering the importance of human needs, attitudes, and
motives in regards to worker motivation and productivity.

C. **Classical Organizational Theory**
1. Emphasizes efficient overall structure.
2. Henri Fayol developed a number of management principles,
including:
  * division of labor.
  * managerial authority over workers.
  * scalar chain of authority.
  * unity of command.
  * subordinate initiative.
3. Max Weber developed the idea of the ideal bureaucracy,
where consistency and fairness were the key factors. Hence
his principles included:
  * formal rules and regulations.
  * impersonal treatment.
  * division of labor.
  * hierarchical structure.
  * authority structure.
  * lifelong career commitment.
4. See Table 1-1. Characteristics of an Ideal Bureaucracy.

D. **Organizational Behavior in the Modern Era**
1. OB emerged as a field in the 1940s with the first doctorate
awarded in 1941.
2. OB was established as a field of study by the late 1950s,

early 1960s.

3. Gordon and Howell reported on business education in 1959 and recommended, among other things, increased attention to the social sciences.

4. OB has grown rapidly, borrowing from other business disciplines.
   - See Figure 1-10. OB: A Hybrid Science.

5. Some current trends in OB are:
   - increased attention to cross-cultural aspects of business.
   - study of ethical and unethical behavior in organizations.
   - a recognition of the importance of the external environment on organizational behavior.
   - expanding to the study of service and information sectors of business.
   - greater work with technology and its impact.

IV. Theory and Research: Tools for Learning about Behavior in Organizations
   A. **Isn't It All Just Common Sense?**
      1. We all have some experience and knowledge about dealing with people.
      2. The importance of OB and the scientific method is that what seems logical is not always true.

   B. **Theory: An Indispensable Guide to Organizational Research**
      1. **Definition** - Theory is a set of statements about the interrelationships among concepts that allow us to predict and explain various processes and events.
         - Prediction and control are essential to establishing a theory.
         - Theories need two things: concepts--goals and motives, and assertions--how those concepts relate.
      2. Definition - Hypotheses are logically derived statements that follow the theory.
      3. The process of developing a theory, corresponding hypotheses, and refining and verifying them is very laborious. Yet theories serve three important functions:
         - they provide a way of organizing information.
         - they help us summarize knowledge in a way that makes sense.
         - they show where we need to do more research.
         - See Figure 1-11. Theory Testing: The Research Process.

   C. **Survey Research: The Correlational Method**
      1. Surveys are the most popular OB research technique.

2. Surveys are questionnaires that help OB researchers gather information.
   - Identify variables of interest.
   - Measure variables as precisely as possible.
   - Determine how variables are related to each other.
   - See Table 1-2. Survey questions designed to measure work attitudes.
3. The study of how variables interrelate is correlation research.
   - This is empirical research.
4. The predictions of the relationships constitute the hypothesis of the research.
5. Once collected, the data must be correlated.
   - See Figure 1-12. Positive and Negative Correlations: What They Mean.
   - Direction may be positive (vary together) or negative (vary in opposite directions).
   - Correlation coefficient measures the strength of the relationship.
   - Multiple regression measures relationship between several variables.
6. Remember correlations do not reveal anything about causation.
   - We know how variables relate.
   - We do not know the cause-effect relationship between them.
   - See Figure 1-13. Correlations: What They Don't Reveal About Causation.

D. **Experimental Research: The Logic of Cause and Effect**
   1. Experimental method is needed to reveal causality.
   2. Experimental method requires which conditions or variables are chosen to be changed to determine their effect on behavior.
   3. The element that the experimenter deliberately manipulates is the independent variable.
   4. The influence of the manipulation is measured on the dependent variable to see how it is influenced by the independent variable.
      - See Figure 1-14. Example of Simple Experimental Results.
   5. The experimental method is built on two ideas:
      - a variable of interest is systematically changed.
      - the effects of those changes are measured.
   6. For the results to be valid, other factors must be held constant--that is unchanged--so that they don't influence the outcome. Hence, there is a preference for laboratory experiments over field experiments, because things are

Instructor's Notes

easier to control.

7. As a consequence, field studies are realistic but may be weak in the area of control.
   - See Figure 1-15. The Trade-offs Between Lab and Field Experimentation.

You be the consultant

1. Students may argue for various types of research, but experimental research is the best choice because they want to know causation.

2. An argument can be made for either lab or field. What's important here is the thoroughness of their design and the rationale students offer for choosing lab or field. a) Have they identified important independent variables? b) How will they measure the changes in the dependent variable? c) Are they cognizant of the trade-offs? d) Why do they think one set of trade-offs is better made than the other?

Instructor's Notes

E. **Qualitative Research: Naturalistic Observation and the Case Method**
   1. Along with quantitative research, there is qualitative research--nonempirical, descriptive techniques based on observation.
   2. **Definition** - naturalistic observation is simply watching people in their working environment.
      - Observe behavior before and after an event, announcement, etc., to note differences.
   3. **Definition** - participant observation involves joining the observed group and working as an insider.
   4. Observational research has some advantages.
      - It doesn't disturb the working routine.
      - Almost anyone can be trained to use it.
   5. Observational research has some drawbacks.
      - It is subjective.
      - Involvement in the organization makes impartiality difficult.
      - Most of what's observed is routine, it is too easy to over emphasize the unique or unusual happening.
   6. **Definition** - case method involves writing detailed accounts of events in an actual organization.
      - Done in order to draw learnings that can be applied to other organizations and circumstances.
      - Built from careful interviewing and data collection over some time.
   7. Its limitations.
      - May only get a partial picture.
      - It may be difficult or impossible to generalize to another organization.
      - The potential for bias is high.

Summary and Review

Questions for Discussion

1. How can the field of organizational behavior contribute to both the effective functioning of organizations and to the well-being of individuals? Are these goals inconsistent? Why or why not?

    Answer - The fact that OB applies a systematic structure, the scientific method, to practical managerial problems makes it a valuable tool for managers. They have a repeatable way to tackle organizational and human problems. Second, the fact that OB looks at all three levels of the organization--individual, group, and organizational--enhances its ability to integrate the goals of people and the organization. Since organizational behavior focuses on improving organizational functioning through people, goal compatibility is not a problem.

2. Explain the following statement: "People influence organizations, and organizations influence people."

    Answer - The answer will depend on the student. Generally, since organizations consist of people and people require organizations to accomplish their goals, their very natures are intertwined. People make an organization's culture and the culture shapes the people.

3. What is the "contingency approach" and why is it so popular in the field of OB today?

    Answer - The fact that there are no success formulas for managing people or organizations. Motivation and leadership strategies depend on the contingencies of the particular event or time. While this approach can be frustrating, it leads to greater accuracy in problem solving but each situation is dealt with on the basis of its elements and not solved according to some universally applied plan.

4. Explain how the field of organizational behavior stands to benefit by taking a global perspective. What would you say are the major challenges associated with such a perspective?

    Answer - It helps the field and the individual manager better manage the growing diversity in the workforce. It raises an appreciation for, and understanding of, other cultures. The changing economic picture in the world, the growing diversity of the workplace, and the changing of the very nature of work are all challenges facing OB.

5. Kurt Lewin, a famous social scientist once said, "There is nothing as applied as good theory." Explain how this statement is applicable to the study of organizational behavior.

    Answer - The answer will depend on the student. Basically an OB specialist needs good theory skills in order to construct the research models needed to solve specific problems. The approach chosen, survey, experiment, observation, and how the research is designed are based on the ability to theorize and develop hypotheses.

6. Under what conditions would it be advisable to learn about organizational behavior by using survey research as opposed to experimental research?

    Answer - When an OB specialist needs to deal with a broad range of issues. Survey research is easier to administrate, easily quantifiable, and subject to sophisticated statistical analysis. It is also easier and less expensive to conduct that experimental research. It can help researchers see the relationships between attitudes and behavior.

7. The Hawthorne studies inadvertently revealed a great deal about behavior in organizations despite flaws in the way the research was conducted. Using your knowledge of the experimental method, describe some of the weaknesses of the Hawthorne studies and ways they may have been alleviated.

    Answer - The researchers had a too narrowly defined hypothesis. They were so committed to scientific management they were blind to other explanations. The question was over-simplified. They needed to better identify their independent variable. When its manipulation or non-manipulation didn't work as expected, they should have sought better controls. Other elements, i.e., attention, weren't accounted for or controlled. They misidentified what independent variable affected their dependent variable.

Case in Point: GEs New Washer Cleans Up Appliance Park

1. Would you say that GE was using the Theory X or Theory Y approach at Appliance Park? What is the basis of this assessment?

    Answer - They are using Theory Y because they involved employees at all levels, they gave employees responsibility and let them make decisions in the work redesign, management and labor clearly worked together on the project, and every effort was made to communicate what was happening and why to all employees.

2. How might a proponent of scientific management attempt to increase efficiency at Appliance Park? What would be the strengths and weaknesses of this approach?

    Answer - In some ways scientific management was used. Where processes were made easier, such as eliminating the overhead lifting) where processes were made safer (the automating of painting) and the very fact that numerous processes were redesigned involved the principles of finding the best way to do the job. The strengths of this approach are enumerated in the above. The weakness is that it tends to make people part of the equipment and less human. It would have been a bit more top down and might well have resulted in a labor/management battle over eliminated jobs, since efficiency, not relationships, is primary in its process.

3. How could scientific research be conducted to determine the impact of the newly designed jobs on GE's employees? Identify a specific research question and an approach that could be taken to answer it.

    Answer - Students can offer a variety of responses. Their justifications are as important as their answers. Basically, survey research can measure attitudes. Managers might want to know how the job redesign has affected employee commitment to GE. Experimental research can assess productivity and quality. Managers could evaluate how the changes have impacted the defect level on production. Observational research could be used to evaluate employee performance before and after the 43 initiatives.

Skills Portfolios
Experiencing Organizational Behavior

Testing Your Assumptions about People at Work
1. Before students read and complete the series of questions, have them write down which management theory they a) endorse and b) think they use. Depending on the sophistication of your students, some will understand that they may well do something different than what they'd like.

2. Explain to the students they need to make their best choice, even in cases where they don't agree with either answer or perhaps they like both answers.
3. The exercise is a real eye opener for students. Often they realize that their actual beliefs and behaviors don't match what they know to be the 'right or correct' answer in dealing with people. Encourage students to see this as an awareness exercise, not a judgment on them, especially if they turn out to be Theory X managers!
4. About ten minutes into the exercise check to see if more time is needed. Encourage the students to choose based on their first reaction rather than lengthy reflection.

Scoring
1. Walk through an example of scoring on an overhead. It's often helpful if you have an overhead or use the blackboard to show students how to score their answers.

Questions for Discussion
1. Before leading the discussion have students answer the questions for themselves.
2. Try having the students answer the questions in reverse order. This will lessen the 'threat' to students who discover they really are Theory X managers.
3. When answering Question #3, strive to get specific incidents and help the students talk about how these incidents affected them. Often they will see their theories of management are reactions to how they've been treated.
4. With Question #2, ask students to think of specific incidents where they've managed other people. For some students these will be occasions when they were planning a party, leading a study group, etc. These situations are as valid as any work-related experience. Have the student share the incident first, ask the class whether that was a Theory X or Y situation, then have the student report what he/she thought the incident showed.
5. For Question #1, I'd just ask who got a surprise and why. Don't focus on who's Theory X or Theory Y oriented, because it could induce resistance to later exercises, especially if the students are embarrassed now.

Working in Groups
Common Sense about Behavior in Organizations: Putting It to the Test

1. Ask the students not to look at the answers under question #10. As soon as you ask some will look, but if you tell them not to it will help many students from inadvertently stumbling over the answers and affecting their results.
2. Appoint a recorder for each group. This person will write down the group's answer and report out during the discussion. Tell the recorder to write everyone's name on the recording sheet and that you will collect the record at the end of class. It will keep him/her honest.
3. Walk among the groups and listen to their discussions. This will help them keep focused on the task and will enable you to pick up on any problems and be able to render assistance.

Scoring
1. Ask the recorder to score the team's answers and be prepared to report the score to you.

Questions for Discussion
1. Rather than focus on how well they did, ask the groups for the questions that were the hardest for them. Write the question numbers 1-10 on the board and keep a tally of the hardest questions.
2. Take the question that was the hardest and discuss it first. This process will automatically get discussion going and help you focus it on the areas where the material isn't clear to the students.

Chapter 2 - Work in the Twenty-First Century: The Changing World of People and Organizations

Learning Objectives

After reading the chapter, you should be able to:

1. Describe the impact of *globalization* of the economy on the operation of organizations.
2. Explain how the cultural differences between people from various nations may account for different organizational behaviors.
3. Understand the nature of *diversity* in today's organizations & things that are done to capitalize on it.
4. Appreciate the impact of various trends in working arrangements, including *downsizing, outsourcing,* the *contingency workforce, virtual corporations,* and *telecommuting.*
5. Describe the various approaches that today's organizations are taking to improve the quality of their goods and services, such as *total quality management* and *reengineering.*
6. Explain why unethical behavior occurs in organizations and what can be done to prevent it.

Chapter Contents

	Page
Introduction	34
I. Globalization and Culture: Today's International Organizations	35
A. Organizations in the Global Arena	36
B. Culture and Its Impact	40
C. Hofstede's Dimensions of Culture	42
II. The Shifting Demographics of the Workforce: Trends Toward Diversity	44
A. Two Philosophies of Diversity: The Melting Pot and Cultural Pluralism	44
B. Today's- and Tomorrow's-Highly Diverse Workforce	45
C. Celebrating Diversity: Accommodating and Capitalizing on Pluralism in the Workplace	48
III. Trends in Working Arrangements: New Organizational Forms and Jobs	51
A. Leaner Organizations: Downsizing and Outsourcing	51
B. The Contingency Workforce: "Permanent Temporary" Employees	53
C. The Virtual Corporation: A Network of Temporary Organizations	55
D. Telecommuting: The Demise of the Office	56
IV. The Quality Revolution: Total Quality Management and Reengineering	58
A. "Total Quality Management" A Commitment to Customers	58
B. Reengineering: Starting All Over	60
V. Corporate Social Responsibility: The Ethical Organizations	61
A. Why Does Unethical Organizational Behavior Occur?	62
B. What Can be Done to Promote Ethical Behavior in Organizations?	63
Summary and Review	65
Questions for Discussion	66
Case in Point	66
Skills Portfolio	67
Experiencing Organizational Behavior	67
Working in Groups	67

Chapter Outline

Instructor's Notes

Case Preview: Texas Instruments (TI) is a model company in fostering diversity. From its *Minority Business Development* initiative, where TI assists minority-owned businesses, to its involvement in *Dallas Women's Covenant*, a pledge to meet specific goals for hiring women, TI is in the forefront of corporate diversity efforts. TI also pays attention to all its employees' need to balance work and personal and family responsibilities. These efforts have paid off for TI.

Introduction
1. Companies that stress the strengths of their diverse workforces create better working conditions for their employees.
2. There has been more change at this time in history than in any previous era. In this chapter some of the forces creating this change will be described.
3. This chapter will cover:
   a. several major themes:
      - the trend towards globalization.
      - the changing workforce, the movement toward diversity.
   b. the impact of rapid advances in technology and their impact on the design of jobs and organizations.
   c. the emphasis on quality that is driving today's organizations.
      - Several developments will be showcased.
   d. the ethical aspects of organizational behavior.
      - The determinants of ethical behavior.
      - Examples of ethical behavior will be offered.

I. Globalization and Culture: Today's International Organizations
   Many everyday objects, cars, computers, clothes are composed of components from a variety of companies in many different countries. What role does a country's culture play in shaping the organization?
   - Figure 2-1 represents the special sections in the chapter.

   A. **Organizations in the Global Arena**
      1. Organizations operate within economic systems into which resources are constantly flowing.
      2. Facts:
         - Only 7% of U.S. companies were influenced by foreign competition in the 1960s. 70% are today.
         - Directly or indirectly, international trade accounts for 20% of all jobs in the U.S.
         - For every $1 billion exported by U.S. companies, about 20,000 jobs are created.

3. International trade has grown from $308 billion in 1950 to $3.8 trillion in 1993. This growth is fueled by:
    *   technology drastically lowering transportation and communication costs.
    *   decreasing legal restrictions.
    *   developing nations promoting exports and opening their doors to foreign investment.
    *   International lending which has grown from $324 billion in 1980 to $7.5 trillion in 1991.
    *   Bundesbank and Federal Reserve actions.
    *   **Definition** - <u>Globalization</u> - the process of interconnecting the world's peoples to the cultural, economic, political, technological, and environmental aspects of their lives.

4. Multinational corporations are the primary vehicles driving globalization.
    *   300 largest MNCs account for 1/4 of world's productive assets.
    *   100 largest MNCs are valued at $3.1 trillion.
    *   There are 35,000 MNCs throughout the world.
    *   See Figure 2-2. Ten largest Nonfinancial MNCs.
    *   **Definition** - <u>expatriates</u> - are citizens of one country who live and work in another.

5. Economic interdependence, countries' economies are becoming intertwined.
    *   9% of U.S. companies are foreign-controlled.
    *   14% of Great Britain's companies are foreign-controlled.
    *   17% of Germany's companies are foreign-controlled.
    *   Economic interdependence is especially high among neighboring countries.
    *   **Definition** - <u>North American Free Trade Agreement</u> (NAFTA) is eliminating tariffs between the U.S., Canada, and Mexico.

6. Cultural homogenization is the tendency for people throughout the world to become culturally similar.
    *   The entertainment industry is one example where American films are highly popular in other countries and cultures.
    *   Social movements to strengthen and protect local cultures are arising in other countries.
    *   Cultural homogenization is complex and widespread.
    *   See Figure 2-3.

B. Culture and Its Impact

1. OB's interest in the influence of culture on attitudes and behavior at work.

2. **Definitions**
   - Culture - the set of values, customs, and beliefs that people have in common with other members of a social unit.
   - Multicultural society - is one within which there are many different racial, ethnic, socioeconomic, and generational groups, each with its own culture.
   - Subculture - describes a smaller cultural group operating within a larger, primary cultural group.

3. Culture shock and adjustment. People are often unconsciously affected by culture. Individuals faced with new cultures may become confused and disoriented. Also, when they return to their own culture, or are **repatriated,** they may experience culture shock again.

4. The adjustment process follows a U-curve, moving from High Acceptance to Low Acceptance, back to High Acceptance over time. Culture shock comes from having a narrow view of the world.
   - Figure 2-4. Adjusting to Foreign Culture: The Central Stages.

5. Convergence versus divergence. In the same way narrow views of how to manage people may severely limit understanding behavior in organizations.
   - Convergence hypothesis was the original view of management, holding that good management practices were universal, and the U.S. practices were best.
   - Divergence hypothesis today seeks to understand the behavior of people in their own cultural contexts and adapting management practices accordingly.

C. **Hofstede's Dimensions of Culture**
   1. Hofstede found that national culture was a strong determinant of work attitudes and behavior. He identified four dimensions of culture:
      - individualism/collectivism.
      - power distance.
      - uncertainty avoidance.
      - masculinity/femininity.
   2. Individualism/collectivism describes to what degree people primarily define themselves as individuals or as members of a group.
   3. Power distance describes the degree to which unequal distribution of power is accepted or rejected.
      - In high power distance countries, subordinates would never bypass their superiors.
      - In low power distance countries, people are readily willing to bypass their superiors.

4. Uncertainty avoidance is the degree to which people are threatened by, and attempt to, avoid ambiguous situations.
5. Masculinity/femininity is not gender related but ties to the degree a culture is materialistic, (values assertiveness and the acquisition of money). Feminine cultures emphasize concern for others and relationships.
6. See Figure 2-5. Hofstede's Four Dimension of Culture: A Summary for examples of countries in each category.

II. The Shifting Demographics of the Workforce: Trends Toward Diversity
   A broad range of cultural differences can also be found *within* organizations. In fact, today's workforce is the most diverse in history.

   A. **Two Philosophies of Diversity: The Melting Pot and Cultural Pluralism**
      1. The melting pot analogy described the assimilation of new immigrants for most of the 20th century. The idea was that people from different backgrounds were transformed by a common American culture.
      2. In the mid-1960s the civil rights movement changed that as the idea of cultural pluralism came to the forefront.
         • Its the idea that social harmony does not require assimilation but that peoples' separate identities can be maintained and accepted.
      3. Another concept, valuing diversity, encourages awareness of and respect for different people in the workplace.

   B. **Today's- and Tomorrow's-Highly Diverse Workforce**
      1. Popular TV sitcoms in the 1950s and 1960s pictured the traditional American family. However it's changed today.
         • The high number of women in the workforce has virtually eliminated the distinctions of male "bread winner" and female "care giver."
         • Shifts in immigration have lowered the percentage of people of European descent in the workforce.
         • The workforce is aging significantly.
      2. In the 1950s nearly 64% of the workforce was white male. In 1990 it was 43.1% and by 2005 it will be 38%. Over half of all women are employed, and they constitute slightly less than half the workforce.
         • Civil rights challenged typical stereotypes.
         • Economic changes made it both possible and necessary for them to work.
         • The number of women in the workforce will continue to rise. See Figure 2-7. Women in the Workplace.

3. U.S. immigration policy has favored northern Europe. Now the majority of immigrants are coming from developing nations. White non-Hispanics constitute 78.5% of the workforce in 1990 but will drop to 73% by 2005.
    - See Figure 2-8. Minorities in the Workplace.
4. The aging of the baby boom generation, those born in the years following World War II, is a significant issue.
    - By 2001 the first wave of baby boomers will become "older workers," 55 years of age.

C. **Celebrating Diversity: Accommodating and Capitalizing on Pluralism in the Workplace**
1. Diversity within an organization can be a significant strength if recognized and utilized.
2. **Definition** - <u>diversity training</u> is designed to get employees to recognize, accept, and value people who are different from themselves.
3. Diversity training must be part of a company-wide effort to recognize and accept diversity in order to be of value.
4. Flexible work arrangements is one way to accommodate the diversity of lifestyles.
    - Flextime programs give employees some discretion over their working hours. These programs have been well received and tied to productivity improvements and decreases in absenteeism.
    - Compressed workweeks permit employees to work fewer but longer days.
    - Job sharing is one way to manage part-time work. Pairs of employees share one job.
    - Voluntary reduced work time programs allow employees to reduce the amount of time they spend on the job, typically 10-20%, with a proportional reduction in pay.
    - Flexplace policies allow employees to perform part of their work from home.
5. Support facilities is a proactive way for companies to address the growing needs of employees.
    - Child-care facilities.
    - Elder-care facilities.
    - Personal support policies are a wide variety of efforts from transportation to high school equivalency classes, etc.
6. All these programs are expensive but companies are convinced they work, and in some cases, they actually save money. In one case, AT&T found it was much cheaper to grant unpaid parental leave than to replace the employee.

III. <u>Trends in Working Arrangements: New Organizational Forms and Jobs</u>

The industrial revolution established the process of people performing tasks within a hierarchical arrangement called an organization. That era is closing as organizations change the way work is done and their structures for doing it.

A. **Leaner Organizations: Downsizing and Outsourcing**
    1. Technology helps fewer people do more work. Some processes like infomating are happening so fast as to change the very nature of work. Key terms:
        - <u>Automation</u> is the replacing of people with machines.
        - <u>Infomating</u> is the process of workers' manipulating products by placing data between themselves and the product.
        - <u>Downsizing</u> is more than laying people off. Its primary purpose is to adjust the number of employees needed to perform the same tasks or the same amount of work.
        - <u>Outsourcing</u> is another restructuring tool. Companies hire outside companies to perform the work.
        - <u>Core competency</u> is what the firm does not outsource, because it is what the company does best.
    2. While these strategies sometimes create great trauma for workers, in other cases the changes are relatively transparent. Some of these techniques, particularly outsourcing, are criticized as hollowing out companies. Nevertheless, nearly 30% of American manufacturers outsource over half of their manufacturing.

B. **The Contingency Workforce: "Permanent Temporary" Employees**
    1. This strategy is simply hiring employees as they are needed for limited periods of time to supplement the regular workforce. This gives companies great flexibility and speed in adjusting their staffing needs.
    2. Evidence of the trend.
        - 899,000 of the new jobs created from 1990 to 1995 were contigency jobs.
        - The largest employer in the U.S., Manpower, Inc., is a temporary agency with 600,000 employees--200,000 more than GM.
        - There are over 7,000 temporary employment firms in the U.S.
        - Charles Handy, a British consultant, believes the corporation of the future will be almost entirely comprised of contingency workers.
    3. There are downsides to contingency work.
        - Employees frequently do not receive benefits.
        - Wages tend to be lower.

- It can be very stressful for people to not have permanent jobs they can depend on.
- Sometimes tension exists between permanent employees with their higher wages and benefits and temporary workers performing the same tasks.
- Sometimes the training costs, etc., for temporary workers offset any wage/benefit savings.

4. See Figure 2-10. Contingency Workers: What Kinds of Jobs do they do?
5. Employers are finding a need for better educated people with high skills. There has been considerable growth among knowledge workers.
   - The most successful workers in the future will be those whose academic and technical training best fits the jobs of the future.

C. **The Virtual Corporation: A Network of Temporary Organizations**
   1. The concept is simply the putting together of the core competencies of several organizations.
      - **Definition** - virtual corporation - a highly flexible temporary organization formed by a group of companies that join forces to exploit a specific opportunity.
   2. An example of such an operation would be the organization and production of a rock concert tour where one company makes travel arrangements, another handles lighting, etc.

D. **Telecommuting: The Demise of the Office**
   1. Is one way to cut down on environmental pollution and wasted time commuting.
      - **Definition** - telecommuting is the use of communications technology to enable work to be performed from remote locations, such as home.
      - It is an essential element of Flexplace policies.
   2. Important facts.
      - There are 7.6 million telecommuters, which is expected to rise to 25 million by the year 2000.
      - 78% of Fortune 500 companies perform significant amounts of their work off-site.
      - 77% of telecommuters work for small firms.
   3. Telecommuting has pluses and minuses.
      - IBM's Chicago office has gone mobile saving 55% of its real estate space, with 85% of employees saying they don't want to go back to a traditional office.

You be the consultant

1. Selling has long used telecommuting, since the sales person's job is to be out of the office and in front of the customer. Students should see telecommuting as a natural solution. Possible benefits: more time in front of customers, lower real estate costs for company, etc. Downside: higher sales expenses--travel costs, equipment to telecommute, harder to manage workers, etc.

2. Sales people have families like any other workers. Add to the situation description by suggesting types of sales forces--i.e., a middle-aged married workforce, younger, single, college-educated sales force, etc.--and have students suggest support facilities/policies that match the type of sales force. Students need to realize that support facilities need to match the specific needs of the employees.

Instructor's Notes

- Some employees have a hard time not having contact with other employees.
- Telecommuting does not lend itself to some types of work.
- You have to have the right person, self-directed, thoroughly trained, with the proper working environment.
- Compensation is also an issue as companies try to decide how to pay workers for their efforts.

IV. The Quality Revolution: Total Quality Management and Reengineering

In the past customers could do little about shoddy quality products. Then the Japanese introduced alternative, high quality products and the quality race began. The quality revolution has forced those companies who want to be the best to relentlessly pursue quality.

A. **"Total Quality Management"–A Commitment to Customers**

1. **Definition** - total quality management (TQM) is an organizational strategy for improving customer satisfaction by developing techniques to carefully manage output quality.
   - W. Edwards Deming is the best-known advocate of TQM.
   - Successful TQM requires an organization-wide commitment to the program.
2. **Definition** - benchmarking - is the process of comparing one's services and products to the best from other firms. It is a key ingredient to TQM.
3. Another key is to instill a concern for quality throughout the organization.
   - **Definition** - quality control audit is the careful examination of how well they are meeting standards.
4. The Malcolm Baldridge Award was established in 1987 by the U.S. Congress to honor companies' quality efforts. The goal of the award is to promote quality achievements.

- See Table 2-1 for the list of winners.

B. **Reengineering: Starting All Over**
1. Described as the hottest trend in management by some, it was started by Michael Hammer and James Champy.
   - **Definition** - reengineering is the fundamental rethinking and radical redesign of business processes to achieve drastic improvements in performance.
2. Reengineering is not a 'fix-it' program but a starting from scratch, looking at the fundamental way things are done.
3. The focus of reengineering is the customer. How can value be added for the customer?
   - Text offers IBM as an example.

V. Corporate Social Responsibility: The Ethical Organizations
Ethics have always been a concern for companies. There is no period in history that does not have its sordid tales of misdeeds. An important change has been the public's unwillingness to tolerate such behavior anymore.
A. **Why Does Unethical Organizational Behavior Occur?**
1. One reason is that organizations often reward behavior that violates ethical standards. Consider corporate reactions to officials who pay bribes and to whistleblowers. Too often the whistleblowers have the greater fear of negative consequences.
2. Some organizations develop counternorms, accepted practices that are contrary to prevailing ethical standards.
   - Figure 2-14 describes Societal Norms vs. Organizational Counternorms.
3. Stonewalling is not cooperating, willingly hiding relevant information in investigations.
4. A bottom-line mentality that makes financial success the only important value also contributes.
5. An exploitative mentality that encourages "using" people in a way that promotes stereotypes and undermines empathy and compassion.
6. A Madison Avenue mentality argues that anything is right if the public can be convinced it's right.
7. All in all, unethical behavior isn't hard to spot. It happens because of various mentalities that encourage it. But some argue that it is becoming unprofitable to be unethical.

B. **What can be done to Promote Ethical Behavior in Organizations?**
1. The authors suggest an individual approach, a testing of each decision a manager makes by asking:
   - Is it right?

Instructor's Notes

- Is it fair?
- Is it purely selfish?
- How would you feel if others found out about it?

2. Second, develop a code of ethics for the organization.
3. Third, conduct an ethics audit, assess the morality of employee behavior.
4. The process ends with another individual step, *challenge your rationalizations about ethical behavior*. Are you using any of these rationalizations?
   - Convincing yourself that something is morally acceptable because it is legally acceptable.
   - Convincing yourself that something is right just because it benefits you.
   - Convincing yourself that something is right because you will never get caught.
   - Convincing yourself that something is right because it helps the company.

Summary and Review

Questions for Discussion

1. Based on the material in this chapter, argue for or against the following statement, "Technology has made the world smaller culturally." Explain your answer.

   Answer - The ability to more easily trade, travel, and communicate across borders due to technology permits both the experiencing of other cultures and the sharing of cultures. The exportation of entertainment, movies, music, etc., exposes other countries to the exporting country's culture. See the discussion of cultural homogenization beginning on page 39.

2. In what ways can we expect the demographics of the workforce to change in the years ahead?

   Answer - There will be increasing pluralism as the number of ethnic minorities in the workforce increases. More women will enter the workforce. The size and influence of the white and male segments of the workforce will decrease. There will be an increasing use of diversity training.

3. In what ways can training help people who are looking to become successful in tomorrow's leaner organizations?

   Answer - First, diversity training which helps employees to recognize, accept, and value people different from themselves will enable employees to work more effectively. Second, technology helps fewer people do more work. Some processes like infomating are happening so fast as to change the very nature of work. Consequently, employers are finding a need for better educated people with high skills. There has been considerable growth among knowledge workers. The most successful workers in the future will be those whose academic and technical training best fits the jobs of the future.

4. How has technology created flexibility in the workplace?
    Answer - The infomating of work, the ability to telecommute through the use of computers, faxes, modems, etc., is eliminating the need for large central office complexes and workers commuting every day to one location to work.

5. What steps are organizations taking to eliminate mediocrity and to become as quality-minded as possible?
    Answer -A firm can adopt a total quality management (TQM) program, an organizational strategy for improving customer satisfaction by developing techniques to carefully manage output quality. They can start benchmarking, the comparing of one's services and products to the best from other firms, which is a key ingredient to TQM. Another key is to instill a concern for quality throughout the organization. They can initiate quality control audits, carefully examining how well they are meeting standards. They could even implement reengineering, a fundamental rethinking and radical redesign of business processes to achieve drastic improvements in performance.

6. If someone said, "Some people are unethical and there's nothing you can do to change them," what would you say? Do you agree or disagree with this statement as it applies to behavior in organizations? Why or Why not?
    Answer - Students' answers will vary. Basically look for the student's understanding of what organizational elements encourage unethical behavior and what the four suggestions from the text are for encouraging ethical behavior.

Case in Point: Differences in Understanding

1. What features of the deal between Pixar and Disney appear to be responsible for the success of their virtual corporation?
    Answer - They tapped the strengths of each. Pixar's understanding and use of computer animation, Disney's creative ability and its great marketing strength.

2. In the future, what kinds of problems would you expect to occur in this virtual corporation?
    Answer - If Disney learns what Pixar does, it may want to do it on its own. Pixar may want to make its own movie projects.

3. What do you think might happen to the arrangement between Pixar and Disney as each of these companies also enter into agreements with other organizations?
    Answer - Conflicts in the scheduling of projects, insufficient resources to manage multiple projects, a problem with sharing of proprietary, confidential information.

Skills Portfolios
Experiencing Organizational Behavior
Are You More Ethical Than the Average Manager? Don't Be So Sure!
1. Below are the two short instruments your text suggests you make up. Copy each on a separate half sheet of paper.
2. Follow the directions in the text for their administration.

Ethical instrument

For each of the following statements, indicate by using the scale below, how willing you think <u>most managers</u> would be to perform the action indicated if it were necessary to protect their jobs.

0 = Always   1 = Usually   2 = Sometimes   3 = Rarely   4 = Never

_____ 1.   Keep negative information from a superior.

_____ 2.   Lie about facts in a performance report.

_____ 3.   Distort information in a financial statement.

_____ 4.   Blame a subordinate for one's own mistakes.

_____ 5.   Break union rules so as to cut costs.

_____ 6.   Authorize the use of deceptive marketing techniques.

_____ 7.   Exaggerate figures on an expense report.

_____ 8.   Payoff an inspector to avoid making costly repairs to already safe equipment.

Ethical instrument

For each of the following statements, indicate by using the scale below, how willing you think <u>you</u> would be to perform the action indicated if it were necessary to protect your jobs.

0 = Always   1 = Usually   2 = Sometimes   3 = Rarely   4 = Never

_____ 1.   Keep negative information from a superior.

_____ 2.   Lie about facts in a performance report.

_____ 3.   Distort information in a financial statement.

_____ 4.   Blame a subordinate for one's own mistakes.

_____ 5.   Break union rules so as to cut costs.

_____ 6.   Authorize the use of deceptive marketing techniques.

_____ 7.   Exaggerate figures on an expense report.

_____ 8.   Payoff an inspector to avoid making costly repairs to already safe equipment.

Scoring
1. Score as directed.

Questions for Discussion
1. Be very careful in managing this class discussion. Some students may get a shock, you may get a shock, as to the level of ethical standards in the class. Recent research show that business students are highly concerned with ethical behavior but tend to score very low on ethical tests. The "bottom-line" mentality is very prevalent in classrooms today.
2. Focus on the implications of the results. Before conducting the exercise, think through the practical implications for several common experiences your students might have and use these to facilitate the implications portion of the discussion. For example:
   - A local fast food restaurant manager uses meat that may have been left out of refrigeration a little too long because he has to cut costs.
   - A garage uses lower costs and lower quality brake components when repairing your car's brakes, because it will increase profitability 10%.
   - A local small retailer does not make social security withholding deposits or pay its workmen's compensation taxes, because it needs that cash to keep operating.
   - Your example
   - Your example
   - Your example

<u>Working in Groups</u>
Baldridge Award Winners: What Makes Them So Special?
1. No further directions. Conduct the exercise as directed in the text.
2. Be aware that this exercise could take a great deal of time. It is quite worthwhile if done well. Consider what incentive you might offer students to encourage a 'quality' performance.

Questions for Discussion
1. Select two or three students to record responses on the blackboard, this will free you to focus on facilitating the discussion.
2. Warn the students before hand that you will go round-robin, asking each group to give one response for each question. This will keep all the groups participating and keep any one group from dominating the class.
3. Use the round-robin process with each of the questions.
4. Use Question #4 only after you've completed the first three. It is significantly different in content and focus and is much more of an opinion question than the first three.

Chapter 3 - Perception and Learning Understanding and Adapting to the Work Environment

Learning Objectives

After reading the chapter, you should be able to:

1. Define social perception and indicate its relevance to organizational behavior.
2. Explain how the attribution process helps us to understand the causes of others' behavior
3. Appreciate the various sources of bias in social perception and how they may be overcome.
4. Understand how the process of social perception operates in the context of performance appraisals, employment interviews, and the cultivation of corporate images.
5. Explain the concept of learning and describe how it operates in organizations.
6. Describe the concepts of operant conditioning and observational learning.
7. Appreciate how principles of learning are involved in organizational programs involving training, organizational behavior management, and discipline.

Chapter Contents

	Page
Introduction	71
I. Social Perception: The Process of Understanding Others	72
II. The Attribution Process: Judging the Causes of Others' Behavior	73
A. "Making Correspondent Inference" Using Acts to Judge Dispositions	73
B. Causal Attribution of Responsibility" Answering the Question, "Why?"	75
III. The Imperfect Nature of Social Perception: Bias and How to Overcome It	76
A. Perceptual Biases: Systematic Errors in Perceiving Others	76
B. Stereotypes: Fitting Others Into Categories	79
C. Overcoming Bias in Social Perception: Some Guidelines	81
IV. Perceiving Others: Organizational Applications	82
A. Performance Appraisals: Making Formal Judgments About Others	82
B. Impression Management in the Employment Interview: Looking Good to Prospective Employers	83
C. Corporate Image: Impression Management by Organizations	85
V. Learning: Adapting to the World Around Us	86
A. Operant Conditioning: Learning Through Rewards and Punishments	87
B. Observational Learning: Learning by Initiating Others	90
VI. Applications of Learning in Organizations	92
A. Training: Learning and Developing Job Skills	92
B. Organizational Behavior Management: Positively Reinforcing Desirable Organizational Behaviors	95
C. Discipline: Eliminating Undesirable Organizational Behaviors	98
Summary and Review	102
Questions for Discussion	103

Case in Point   103
Skills Portfolios   104
    Experiencing Organizational Behavior   104
    Working in Groups   104

Chapter Outline

Instructor's Notes

Case Preview: Example of Taco (TAY-co) a manufacturer that offers educational opportunities to its employees at its cost. This has helped the company weather bad economic times, lower costs, and reduce turnover.

Introduction
1. Taco has helped employees learn new skills while enhancing the company's image. This is an example of one way perceptions are formed.
2. Perception is simply a process based on learning. You learn about others by interacting with them, you form perceptions.
3. Learning is more than formal classes and education. Everyday activities that provide information are part of the learning process.

I. Social Perception: The Process of Understanding Others
    Definition - Perception - is the process of making sense out of the vast array of sensory inputs. It involves the active processing of information.
    A. Perception is very important in OB. It helps us to understand who the people around us are and why they do what they do.
        1. **Definition** - social perception - is the task of combining, integrating, and interpreting information about others to gain an accurate understanding of them.
        2. **Definition** - attribution - is the way people come to judge the underlying causes of others' behavior.

II. The Attribution Process: Judging the Causes of Others' Behavior
    A. **Making Correspondent Inference: Using Acts to Judge Dispositions.**
        1. We often want to know what people are like. Generally, we do this by observing their behavior and then inferring their traits.
            * **Definition** - correspondent inferences - are judgments about what someone is liked based on what we observe about him/her.
            * See Figure 3-2. Correspondent Inferences: Judging Dispositions Based On Behavior.
        2. This process seems simple enough and is sometimes accurate, but may be inaccurate because:

- behavior often has many causes.
- individuals are sometimes affected by external forces.
- people tend to conceal some of their traits.

<u>Instructor's Notes</u>

3. Observations can be made more accurate by:
   - focusing on behavior in situations where a person's behavior is limited by expectations.
   - focusing on behavior with only one apparent cause.

B. **"Causal Attribution of Responsibility" Answering the Question, "Why?"**
   1. It is generally important to determine if behavior is attributable to internal or external causes.
   2. How we decide that someone's behavior is internally or externally motivated is answered, to some degree, by Kelley's theory of causal attribution.
   3. To understand Kelley's theory first you must understand key terms:
      - <u>Consensus</u> - the extent to which other people behave in the same manner as the person we're judging.
      - <u>Consistency</u> - the extent to which the person we're judging acts the same way in similar situations.
      - <u>Distinctiveness</u> - the extent to which this person behaves in the same manner in other contexts.
   4. If the person's behavior is high in consensus, consistency, and distinctiveness, we tend to conclude external causes are at work.
   5. If the person's behavior is low in consensus, high in consistency, and low in distinctiveness we tend to conclude that internal causes are at work.
      - Text gives an example on page 76.
      - See Figure 3-3. Kelley's Theory of Causal Attribution: A Summary.

III. <u>The Imperfect Nature of Social Perception: Bias and How to Overcome It</u>
   A. **Perceptual Biases: Systematic Errors in Perceiving Others**
      1. Some errors in judgment reflect bias due to the way we think about others in general. These are perceptual biases. There are five such biases.
         - The <u>fundamental attribution</u> error occurs when behavior is attributed to internal causes regardless of the evidence.
         - The <u>halo effect</u> is when a former impression, negative or positive, taints everything we observe the person do.
            - See Figure 3-4. The Halo Effect: A Demonstration.

- Similar-to-me effect results when pople perceive individuals like themselves more favorably than others.
- First-impression error, whatever our first impression, that is our opinion and judgment about the person regardless of other evidence and behavior. This can often be very subtle.
  - Figure 3-5. First-Impression Error: A Summary.
- Selective Perception refers to the tendency for individuals to focus on certain aspects of the environment while ignoring others.

B. **Stereotypes: Fitting Others Into Categories**
  1. These ideas are what come to mind when we see particular people or groups of people. Most often they are negative, and they are often assumptions.
  2. We rely on stereotypes, because it saves us cognitive effort, and it helps us deal with the multitudes of people we come in contact with--it is mental shorthand.
  3. In organizations stereotypes may hinder the firm by eliminating a good job candidate or limiting a person's opportunities.
     - Sometimes the effect of stereotypes can be very subtle.

C. **Overcoming Bias in Social Perception: Some Guidelines**
  1. Misperceptions are not often the result of malice but rather because we are imperfect processors of information. We can reduce or eliminate stereotypes and misperceptions by:
     - not overlooking the external causes of behavior.
     - identifying and confronting personal stereotypes.
     - evaluating people on objective facts.
     - avoiding rash judgments.

IV. Perceiving Others: Organizational Applications
  A. **Performance Appraisals: Making Formal Judgments About Others**
  1. Performance appraisal is simply the evaluation of someone's job performance by another.
     - Done annually or semi-annually.
     - Used to determine raises, promotions, and training needs.
  2. The process should be rational and fair but bias may be introduced by:
     - the degree of consistency of performance with expectations.
     - employees cultivating their relationships with supervisors who by doing them favors tend to receive higher ratings than those who don't.

- employees making themselves look better in the eyes of their supervisor.

B. **Impression Management in the Employment Interview: Looking Good to Prospective Employers**
1. We all do things to control how others see us, attempting to make them see us in the best possible light. Impressions may be based on:
    - subtle behaviors, such as dress and speech patterns.
    - calculated efforts to manipulate others' impressions.
    - self-promotion, the flat assertion that one has the characteristics sought.
    - See Table 3-1. How do Job Applicants Present Themselves Favorably?
2. Use of the various techniques outlined in Figure 3-1 had strong positive results for job candidates.

You be the consultant

1. Your text doesn't present alternative interviewing strategies. If you're familiar with behavioral interviewing, do a mini-lecture. In any case, students should talk about questions that help applicants describe things they've done that demonstrate the required skills or characteristics, and questions or interview techniques that give interviewers the opportunity to observe the desired behaviors or characteristics.

2. Students can raise any of the biases covered on pages 77-79 and stereotyping on page 79-80. The importance here is that the students understand what the bias is and are able to justify why it would affect the interviewer. Students should recall the strategies from page 81 when offering ways to overcome interviewer bias.

C. **Corporate Image: Impression Management by Organizations**
1. Sometimes entire organizations want to cultivate or manage a positive image. Positive corporate image can impact who wants to work there.
2. Corporate images can be affected by:
    - the amount of information people have about the company.
    - advertisements about the company.
    - the company's annual report.
3. See Table 3-2. America's Most Admired Companies.

V. <u>Learning: Adapting to the World Around Us</u>

Globalization and Diversity in Today's Organizations
<u>Saving Face In Japan</u>

1. Discussion of the concept of "shame" in Japan, using individuals' wedding experiences as examples. Keeping up appearance is critical to the Japanese.

<u>Instructor's Notes</u>

A. **Operant Conditioning: Learning Through Rewards and Punishments**

1. Learning is a relatively permanent change in behavior occurring as a result of experience. Learning requires:
   - that some kind of change occur.
   - that the change be more than temporary.
   - experience.

2. **Definition** - <u>operant conditioning</u> - is the principle that our behavior produces consequences, and the way we behave in the future will depend on the consequences. Also called instrumental conditioning.
   - If our conduct has pleasant consequences it will likely be repeated.
   - If our conduct has unpleasant consequences, it will not likely be repeated.
   - This describes the Law of Effect.
   - Concept is based on the work of B.F. Skinner.
   - See Figure 3-8. The Operant Conditioning Process.

3. Reinforcement Contingencies is learning from the effects of our actions.
   - Positive reinforcement results from desirable outcomes.
   - Negative reinforcement or avoidance comes from undesirable outcomes.
   - Punishment or withholding reward can lead to extinction (disappearance) of behavior.
   - Various conditions outlined above are called the contingencies of reinforcement.
   - See Table 3-3. Contingency of Reinforcements: A Summary.

4. Schedules of reinforcement: patterns of administering rewards help us understand how behavior is reinforced or extinguished.
   - Continuous reinforcement means reward is withheld or presented every time behavior occurs.
   - Partial or intermittent reinforcement schedules may follow one of four patterns:
     - <u>fixed-interval</u> - reinforcement is administered the first time desired behavior appears after a specific amount of time.

- variable-interval - reinforcement is administered on a variable schedule, based on some average amount.
- fixed-ratio - reinforcement is administered the first time desired behavior appears after a specified number of such actions have been performed.
- variable-ratio - a variable number of desired responses must elapse between administration of reinforcement.
- See Figure 3-9. Schedules of Reinforcement: A Summary.

B. Observational Learning: Learning by Initiating Others

1. This type of learning by modeling occurs when someone acquires new knowledge vicariously--by observing others. In the process:
   - attention must be paid by learner.
   - learner must retain model's behavior.
   - learner must behaviorally reproduce model's behavior.
   - learner must have motivation to learn from model.
2. This type of learning is common, especially in job-instruction training.

VI. Applications of Learning in Organizations

    A. Training: Learning and Developing Job Skills

1. Training's many forms:
   - apprenticeship programs.
   - executive training programs.
   - corporate universities.

The Ethics Angle

The Tailhook Scandal: Vicariously Reinforcing Unethical Behavior

1. The point is made that not punishing unacceptable behavior is to tacitly approve of the behavior. In this case, by not punishing sexual harassment, the behavior was reinforced, not extinguished.

2. Omission can be as reinforcing as action. Managers need to keep this in mind when they ignore inappropriate, unethical, or illegal behavior because, "it's no big deal," "I just want to keep the peace."

3. Ask students what impact 1) ignoring cheating and then 2) severely punishing cheating--(expulsion) might have on cheating on campus, which according to current news reports, is rampant.

---

2. Principles that make training effective.
   - Participation in the learning process not only enhances the speed of learning but also retention.

- Repetition.
- Transfer of learning involves applying what is learned to the job.
- Feedback provides knowledge of results of one's actions.
  - 360 Degree feedback is the process of using multiple sources to evaluate one individual, often superiors, peers, and subordinates.
  - See Figure 3-12. 360 Degree Feedback: An Overview.

B. **Organizational Behavior Management: Positively Reinforcing Desirable Organizational Behaviors**
1. The administration of rewards selectively to reinforce behavior is the basis of organizational behavior management.
2. Steps to effective organizational behavior management:
   - Pinpoint desired behavior.
   - Perform a baseline audit.
   - Define a criterion standard. ·
   - Choose a reinforcer.
   - Selectively reward desired behaviors.
   - Periodically re-evaluate the program.
3. See Table 3-4. Organizational Behavior Management

The Quest for Quality
Corporate Goliaths Training Corporate Davids

1. In the quest for quality, some larger companies are providing training for their smaller company suppliers to help them improve quality.
2. They've offered various forms of help/training:
- classroom training.
- on-site counseling.
- building efficiencies.
- working one-on-one.
3. Regardless of the approach, big businesses are building their businesses by developing the skills of smaller businesses that they do business with.

C. **Discipline: Eliminating Undesirable Organizational Behaviors**
1. Discipline is the systematic administration of punishment.
2. Progressive discipline bases punishment on the frequency and severity of the infraction

<u>Instructor's Notes</u>

3. Principles of effective discipline:
    - Deliver punishment immediately after the undesirable response occurs.
    - Give moderate levels of punishment - nothing too high or too low.
    - Punish the undesirable behavior, not the person.
    - Use punishment consistently - all the time, for all employees.
    - Clearly communicate the reasons for the punishment given.
    - Do not follow punishment with non-contingent rewards.
4. See Figure 3-13. Conducting a Disciplinary Interview.

Summary and Review

<u>Questions for Discussion</u>

1. <u>Describe an organizational situation in which it would be important to judge whether someone's behavior stems primarily from internal or external causes.</u>

    Answer - Students need to draw from several areas to answer this question. It is important in hiring and managing people so the manager knows what to do to get more of what he/she wants and to extinguish unwanted behavior. It is important in dealing with discipline in order to choose the proper process.

2. <u>How do stereotypes influence the way we judge others in organizations? How may stereotypical judgments be overcome?</u>

    Answer - Stereotypes may lead to errors in judgment about the way we think about others. These ideas are what come to mind when we see particular people or groups of people. Most often they are negative and they are often assumptions. We rely on stereotypes because it saves us cognitive effort, it helps us deal with the multitudes of people we come in contact with, and it is mental shorthand. In organizations, stereotypes may hinder the firm by eliminating a good job candidate or limiting person's opportunities. Sometimes the effect of stereotypes can be very subtle. **There are five stereotyping errors we can make.** 1) <u>The fundamental attribution error</u> occurs when behavior is attributed to internal causes regardless of the evidence. 2) <u>The halo effect</u> is when a former impression, negative or positive, taints everything we observe the person do. 3) <u>Similar-to-me effect</u> results when someone perceives individuals like themselves more favorably than others. 4) <u>First-impression error</u>, whatever our first impression, that is our opinion and judgment about the person regardless of other evidence and behavior. This can often be very subtle. 5) <u>Selective Perception</u> refers to the tendency for individuals to focus on certain aspects of the environment while ignoring others. **We can reduce or eliminate stereotypes** and misperception by: 1) not overlooking the external causes of behavior, 2) identifying and confronting personal stereotypes, 3) evaluating people on objective facts, and 4) avoiding rash judgments.

3. What kinds of things might people do to be able to enhance the impressions they leave on others in organizations?

    Answer - See Table 3-1. How do Job Applicants Present Themselves Favorably?

4. Identify an organizational event in which operant conditioning is used and one in which observational learning is used.

    Answer - Students can name several occasions. Most common will be performance management and training.

5. Name four different schedules of reinforcement and describe how each may be used in organizations.

    Answer - Schedules of reinforcement are patterns of administering rewards. There are two types of patterns, continuous reinforcement--reward is withheld or presented every time behavior occurs, and partial or intermittent reinforcement. Partial or intermittent reinforcement may follow one of four patterns. 1) Fixed-interval - reinforcement is administered the first time desired behavior appears after a specific amount of time. 2) Variable-interval - reinforcement is administered on a variable schedule, based on some average amount. 3) Fixed-ratio - reinforcement is administered the first time desired behavior appears after a specified number of such actions have been performed. 4) Variable-ratio - a variable number of desired responses must elapse between administration of reinforcement. See Figure 3-9 for a summary of reinforcement schedules.

6. Describe how principles of reinforcement and punishment are used in organizational behavior management programs and disciplinary programs.

    Answer - The selective administration of rewards to reinforce behavior is the basis of organizational behavior management. The steps to effective organizational behavior management are: 1) pinpoint desired behavior, 2) perform a baseline audit, 3) define a criterion standard, 4) choose a reinforcer, 5) selectively reward desired behaviors, and 6) periodically re-evaluate the program. See Table 3-4. Organizational Behavior Management Programs: Some Success Stories. When dealing with punishment, the principles of effective discipline demonstrate organizational behavior management. 1) Deliver punishment immediately after the undesirable response occurs. 2) Give moderate levels of punishment - nothing too high or too low. 3) Punish the undesirable behavior, not the person. 4) Use punishment consistently - all the time, for all employees. 5) Clearly communicate the reasons for the punishment given. 6) Do not follow punishment with non-contingent rewards. See Figure 3-13. Conducting a Disciplinary Interview: Some Key Steps.

Case in Point: Differences in Understanding

1. What other inexpensive training methods do you think Connors Communications might introduce to supplement those it is currently using?

    Answer - Connors Communications seems to be doing the right things. Students may offer more one-on-one coaching, the use of a reinforcement schedule of on-the-job behavior, perhaps an apprenticeship program, and maybe a feedback program.

2. <u>In what ways is the company's small size both a strength and a weakness when it comes to training</u>?
    Answer - The weaknesses are obvious: small budget, limited training resources, insufficient employees to justify any effort that will bring economy of scale. Strengths--forced innovation and use of technology. More personal attention and personal knowledge of employees, therefore better targeted training.

3. <u>Much of what is done at Connors Communication involves sharing existing knowledge among the employees. What can be done to help bring in new sources of information?</u>
    Answer - Answers will vary by student. They might suggest the use of technology, i.e. the Internet and computers. They may suggest tuition reimbursement, letting employees go to the local community college. Etc. Watch for inappropriate answers, i.e., start their own corporate college, etc.

4. <u>Drawing upon the principles of learning discussed in the text, what would you do to enhance the effectiveness of training at Connors Communications?</u>
    Answer - Answers will vary, but generally, students should suggest more interactive training (participation), repeat sessions (repetition), more on-the-job training, or the giving of assignments to cause employees to use the training in their jobs (transfer of training), and some sort of testing (feedback).

<u>Skills Portfolios</u>
<u>Experiencing Organizational Behavior</u>

Identifying Occupational Stereotypes
1. Consider using the instrument before students read the chapter or you lecture on its content/principles. Give the instrument to students with just the instructions. Do not give the introductory comments.

2. You may use this as a group exercise, as it is written in the text. Or use it as an individual exercise and large class discussion. Using it as the latter provides variety and permits you to call on and motivate any students you feel might be using the group exercises to "tune out of the class." Remember omission is as reinforcing as action.

3. Whenever you give the instrument, review the rating scale. Someone always gets it backwards if you don't.

4. Be sure to appoint a recorder/reporter. Advise the students you will call on different groups to share their answer to a selected question to start the discussion.

Scoring
1. Once everyone has completed the instrument, have them score it themselves by totaling the number of points. A profession with all the characteristics could receive a maximum of 20. The lowest number would be a 1.

2. <u>If you use it as a class exercise do the following. Otherwise move to the discussion questions.</u> Write the six professions on the board. Under each write 25, 20, 15, 10, 5. Ask the class how many people scored each profession at 25, the between 20 and 25, and so forth. Count the responses and mark the

number next to the appropriate number. This will reveal the general tendencies of the class prior to the discussion.

Questions for Discussion
1. Work through the questions, calling on a different group each time to lead the discussion with the groups' response. This keeps the groups on their toes.
2. Emphasize Question #3. Use the first two questions to warm everyone up but then use #3 to get at whether students actually know someone in the profession or if they've formed their impressions from TV, movies, comments by others, etc. Call on selected students to share their specific experiences, cautioning them first to not name the individuals described.
3. Most students will obviously respond to Question #4 that they will stop perpetuating stereotypes. Ask students to share 'surprises' or learnings from hearing others describe their perceptions of these professions. In large classes you probably have students who have either worked with each type of professional or who had parents who are in these professions. Ask students to share how others treatment of the professional was just or unjust based on the stereotypes. What you want to help the students realize is how stereotypes hurt the stereotyped person.

<u>Working in Groups</u>
Role Play: The Disciplinary Interview
1. This a powerful exercise. You need to monitor the role play carefully because students can get into the roles, and depending on personality, could say hurtful things or withdraw from the interaction.
2. Photocopy the Role Sheets and provide only the appropriate copy to each student.
3. Instruct observing students, while the role players are out of the room, to watch for specific things. Have someone keep track of who talks the most, if each step of the model was covered, nonverbal behavior of the supervisor, of the employee, etc. You can also ask certain observing students to be prepared to address specific questions for discussion. This will help focus the student's observation and note taking.
4. Stop the exercise and ask the role playing students for feedback first. Ask the supervisor how it went, what he/she thought of the interaction, etc. Then ask the employee how he/she felt. Then ask why. The supervising student and observing students may receiving some surprising feedback. Often the employee feels far more threatened than those not receiving the supervisor's comments.
5. Consider mixed gender and same gender pairs for the exercise. If you do this you can help students develop sensitivity to gender issues in discipline.

Questions for Discussion
1. Have the observing students give feedback on the specific behaviors you assigned earlier before getting into the discussion questions.
2. Consider letting the role playing students answer each question either first or last in the discussion. If they answer it first, other students' feedback will help them see how accurate their personal observations were. If they answer last, it gives them the opportunity to 'defend' themselves if they receive particularly harsh feedback. Letting them set the stage or defend themselves helps the role players to deal with any feelings they may have or develop that they didn't do such a great job in front of their peers.
3. Reword Question #5. As it is stated, it invites conflict. Better, "how would you suggest the first supervisor might more effectively handle the discipline interview?" "How would you suggest the second supervisor . . . ?" Remember to have the supervisor comment first, how does he/she think he/she might have been more effective.

Chapter 4 - Individual Differences: Personality and Abilities

Learning Objectives

After reading this chapter, you should be able to:

1. Define personality and comment on the question of whether it is stable and real.
2. Identify the "big five" dimensions of personality and explain how they are related to organizational behavior.
3. Explain what is meant by negative affectivity and the Type A behavior pattern.
4. Explain what is meant by the proactive personality and indicate its effects on organizational behavior.
5. Describe the Machiavellian personality and steps you can take to protect against persons showing this trait.
6. Distinguish between the work-related motives of achievement, power, and affiliation.
7. Describe the difference between morning and evening persons and the relevance of these differences to on-the-job behavior.
8. Distinguish between a test's reliability and its validity.

Chapter Contents

	Page
Introduction	108
I. Personality: Its Basic Nature and Role in Organizational Behavior	109
A. Is Personality Real? The Person-Situation Controversy	109
II. Work-Related Aspects of Personality	111
A. The "Big Five" Dimensions of Personality and Organizational Behavior	111
B. Positive and Negative Affectivity: Stable Tendencies to Feel Good or Bad at Work	112
C. The Type A Behavior Pattern: Why Being in a Hurry Can Be Costly to Your Health	113
D. The Proactive Personality: People Who Shape Their Environments	115
E. Self-Efficacy: The "Can-Do" Facet of Personality	117
F. Self-Monitoring: Self-Image Versus Private Reality	118
G. Machiavellianism: Using Others to Get Ahead	121
H. Work-Related Motives: Achievement, Power, and Affiliation	123
I. Morning Persons and Evening Persons	126
III. Abilities: Having What it Takes	127
A. Intellectual Abilities	128
B. Physical Abilities	131
IV. Measuring Individual Differences: Some Basic Methods	131
A. Objective and Projective Tests	131
B. Reliability and Validity: Essential Requirements	132
Summary and Review	134
Questions for Discussion	135
Case in Point	136
Skills Portfolios	136
Experiencing Organizational Behavior	137
Working in Groups	137

Chapter Outline

Case Preview: Dell Computers is a success story built on the personality of Michael Dell. Case reviews how Michael Dell showed the characteristics that have led his company to success at a young age. Despite his successes Michael Dell had to learn from some serious mistakes, and did so.

Introduction
1. Dell's success is based to a large degree on Michael Dell's personality.
2. This chapter will cover:
    a. How personal characteristics play a key role in many aspects of organizational behavior.
    b. A definition of personality.
    c. Consideration of those aspects of personality that are important to organizational behavior.
    d. The mental and physical capabilities necessary to work-related behavior.
    e. How personality is measured and used to make practical organization-related decisions.

I. Personality: Its Basic Nature and Role in Organizational Behavior
All human beings possess a distinct pattern of traits and characteristics not fully duplicated in anyone else. This is **personality**, the unique and relatively stable pattern of behavior, thoughts, and emotions shown by individuals. **Ability** refers to the capacity to perform various tasks or cognitive activities.
A. **Is Personality Real? The Person-Situation Controversy**
    1. Some argue that what consistency we see in behavior is illusionary, we impose it.
    2. Others argue that stable traits do exist and research seems to support their view.
    3. If we grant that personality exists, to what extent do we behave due to personality or situations? Most accept an **interactionist perspective** that behavior is a function of personality and context.
        • Implication some work settings may better fit some personalities than others.
        • This should be considered in hiring.

II. Work-Related Aspects of Personality
A. **The "Big Five" Dimensions of Personality and Organizational Behavior**
    1. There are 17,953 words used to describe personality. These can be combined into 171 distinct traits. Five dimensions continue to emerge from a variety of studies conducted in a variety of ways. Those dimensions are:

Instructor's Notes

- <u>Conscientiousness</u> - a dimension that ranges from careful, thorough, responsible, organized, etc., to irresponsible, disorganized, etc.
- <u>Extroversion - Introversion</u> - the dimension ranges from sociable talkative, assertive, active, to retiring, sober, reserved, and cautious.
- <u>Agreeableness</u> - a dimension that ranges from good-natured, gentle, cooperative, forgiving, and hopeful, to irritable, ruthless, suspicious, etc.
- <u>Emotional Stability</u> - a dimension that ranges from anxious, depressed, angry, emotionally insecure, etc., to calm, enthusiastic, poised and secure.
- <u>Openness to Experience</u> - a dimension that ranges from imaginative, sensitive, intellectual, and polished, to down-to-earth, insensitive, narrow, crude, and simple.

2. Table 4-1. The "Big Five" Dimensions of Personality.
3. Many researchers believe these five dimensions are foundational to personality, and there does seem to be a correlation between them and job success.

B. **Positive and Negative Affectivity: The Stable Tendency to Feel Good or Bad At Work**
   1. Moods may fluctuate rapidly and widely. Traits are more stable and are superimposed over these moods.
      - **Positive affectivity** is the tendency to have an overall sense of well-being, seeing people and events in a positive light.
      - **Negative affectivity** is the tendency to hold negative views of oneself and others.
   2. There is evidence that these difference have an effect on organizational behavior.

<u>You be the consultant</u>

1. The obvious answer is yes, it could be. Students will offer a variety of solutions, most will be fairly superficial. Help the students focus on substantive solutions--redesigning jobs, screening sales people for positive affectivity, etc.

Instructor's Notes

C. **The Type A Behavior Pattern: Why Being in a Hurry Can Be Costly to Your Health**
   1. There seem to be two broad behavioral categories of people:
      - Type A - competitive, irritable, in a hurry.
      - Type B - relaxed, easy-going, noncompetitive.
   2. These behaviors impact health, task performance, and relationships. The discussion of health is postponed to Chapter 7.

3. Type As work harder and faster than Type Bs but do not necessarily do better work. More top executives are Type Bs. Neither type has an advantage in work performance.
4. Type Bs may have an edge in relationships because of Type As' fast-paced irritability.

D. **The Proactive Personality: People Who Shape Their Environments**
1. While events do shape circumstances some people respond actively and try to shape their environment. People high in the **proactive personality** trait:
   - make suggestions.
   - identify opportunities.
   - take action.
2. Crant conducted a study of this trait.
   - See Figure 4-4. The Proactive Personality and Success.
3. These people become *change agents*, people who get results when they are needed most.

E. **Self-Efficacy: The "Can-Do" Facet of Personality**
1. This is the belief in one's own capacity to perform a specific task. We develop these beliefs from:
   - direct experience--feedback from performing similar tasks.
   - vicarious experience--observations of others.
2. When initially acquiring skills, people spend a great deal of time developing self-efficacy beliefs. But with experience this process becomes automatic.
   - See Figure 4-3.
3. The implication is that once a self-efficacy belief is formed, it is highly resistant to change.

F. **Self-Monitoring: Self-Image Versus Private Reality**
1. Individuals who are aware of and willing to change their personal style, depending on who they are interacting with, demonstrate **self-monitoring** skills.
2. High self-monitors do better in boundary spanning activities, communicating and interacting with different groups.
   - They readily adjust their actions to meet the expectations of each group.
3. High self-monitors experience more career success than low self-monitors, probably because of:
   - their willingness to adapt.
   - their ability to emphasize with others.
   - their skill at impression management.
   - their tendency to initiate mentoring relationships, becoming acquainted with higher-level managers.

Instructor's Notes

4.   But high self-monitoring people can be seen as "social chameleons" and viewed as:
- unreliable.
- inconsistent.
- manipulative.

The Organization of the Future
The Potential Benefits of Boosting Self-Efficacy: Helping People Help Themselves
1.   This sidebar should help students see they can change the way they think about themselves and their job/school performance and change it for the better.
2.   Discuss with students how they can have experiences that will build their self-efficacy. One strategy is to have the students pick something they want to do but have not been successful at. Have them set small incremental goals, steps to take. Each one should be easily accomplishable, the next step being slightly more difficult than the previous. While a slow process, it is a process used quite successfully with reticent people in building communication skills, with remarkable success.

Instructor's Notes

G. **Machiavellianism: Using Others to Get Ahead**
1.   Machiavelli recommended several principles for manipulating and using others in his 1513 work.
- Never be humble, always be arrogant.
- Morality and ethics are for the weak.
- It is better to be feared than loved.
2.   This is the "do what ever it takes to get it done" management philosophy. Most don't do this but a few people do. **Machiaveilians** succeed in loosely structured situations where there are few rules.
3   Dealing with High Machs
- Expose them to others. This neutralizes their ability to get ahead by lying and using dirty tricks.
- Pay attention to what others do, not what they say. They will say one thing and do another.
- Avoid situations where they have an edge, such as highly emotional ones or where others are unsure how to proceed.

H. **Work-Related Motives: Achievement, Power, and Affiliation**
1.   Achievement motivation: the quest for excellence refers to the strength of an individual's desire to excel.
- People high in achievement motivation are attracted to moderately difficult tasks and strongly desire feedback on their performance.
- These types of people do tend to succeed in their careers but do not necessarily make good managers because they tend to centralize power.
- See Figure 4-7. Achievement Motivation and Attraction to Organizations.

2. Affiliation and Power Motivation: Two sides of the same coin? The desire for power and the desire for relationships may seem opposites but research shows linkages.
3. People with a Leadership Motivation Pattern (LMP) - high power motivation, low affiliation motivation, and a high degree of self-control - are more successful managers than those without LMP.

I. **Morning Persons and Evening Persons**
   1. The *Circadian rhythm* is the cycle of the times of day when people feel the most alert and energetic.
      - Morning people feel most energetic during the day.
      - Evening people feel more energetic during the night.
   2. This has significant implications for job performance.
      - See Figure 4-9. Circadian Rhythm and Performance.

Globalization and Diversity in Today's Organizations
<u>Achievement Motivation and Economic Growth</u>
1. Discuss with the students the implications of McClelland's study for U.S. internal economic policy.
2. How might these finding's impact organizations' selection processes.
3. What do these findings say about the importance of the individual to a group, an organization, a society?

III. <u>Abilities: Having What it Takes</u>
   A. **Intellectual Abilities**
      1. Is the capacity to perform various cognitive tasks.
      2. Intelligence is simply the ability to think abstractly and to learn readily from experience.
         - **Componential intelligence** involves the ability to think critically and analytically.
         - **Experiential intelligence** involves the ability to pull seemingly unrelated information together to formulate new ideas.
         - **Contextual intelligence** is more practical, "streetwise" intelligence, marking the ability to evaluate a situation and adapt to it.
         - **Emotional intelligence** refers to the ability to perceive and control emotions, our own and others.
      3. Cognitive abilities consist of:
         - **perceptual speed**--the ability to recognize similarities and differences in visual stimuli quickly.
         - **number aptitude**--the ability to work with numbers, quickly and accurately.
         - **spatial visualization**--the ability to imagine how various objects will look when changed in a space.
      4. Memory has several different forms:
         - **semantic memory** - the capacity to store abstract, general knowledge.

- **implicit memory** - the ability to retain information that can't be put into words, such as motor skills.
- **working or short-term memory** - the retention of information you are currently working with.
- See Table 4-3. Memory Systems: An Overview.

5. The connection between memory and age is not proven but largely folklore. While short-term and prospective memory does seem to decline with age, other forms of memory are largely unaffected.

B. **Physical Abilities**
1. Is the capacity to perform various physical actions.
2. Physical abilities are broken into two categories:
   - Strength, the capacity to exert muscular force.
   - Flexibility, the capacity to engage in bodily movement.

IV. Measuring Personality: Some Basic Methods
   A. **Objective and Projective Tests**
   1. **Objective Tests,** such as inventories and questionnaires, are the most widely used.
   2. **Projective Tests,** such as the TAT (Thematic Apperception Test), attempt to assess personality based upon analysis of what the person "projects" of him/herself in response to the test stimuli.
      - See Figure 4-10.

   B. **Reliability and Validity: Essential Requirements**
   1. **Reliability** is the degree to which a test yields stable, consistent scores over time.
   2. **Validity** is the extent to which a test measures what it is supposed to measure.
      - See Figure 4-11. Reliability and Validity: An Overview.

The Ethics Angle
Can Tests Have an Adverse Impact?
1. Be sure students understand the meaning of adverse impact, that it is unintentional discrimination because of the testing process, the test itself, or the results.

Summary and Review

Questions For Discussion

1. Why might two individuals whose personalities are very similar behave differently in a given situation?

   Answer - Because people's behavior is a function of personality and situation. As discussed on self-monitoring, those who have high self-monitoring will adapt more to a situation than others of the same personality but with low self-monitoring.

2. How does a close person-job fit contribute to good performance?

   Answer - People are more productive and more satisfied if there is a good job fit.

3. What is the difference between being in a good mood and having the characteristic of positive affectivity?

   Answer - Moods may fluctuate rapidly and widely. Affectivity is more stable and is superimposed over moods. Positive affectivity is the tendency to have a overall sense of well-being, seeing people and events in a positive light.

4. Suppose that you were hiring someone to perform a job that required very fast performance. Would you prefer a Type A or Type B person? Why?

   Answer - Most students will argue for Type A. Astute students will pick up that you can make an argument for either; for while Type A will work faster, Type B will make fewer errors needing correction and therefore may work just as fast. Help the students avoid falling into stereotyping.

5. In what fields do you think individuals high on the proactivity personality dimension would excel? Why?

   Answer - This tendency can succeed in almost any job, but those where change, persuasion, selling, etc. are important are best. The proactive person's ability to see opportunity, to take charge, to be upbeat all work well in these situations.

6. How does having low self-efficacy interfere with task performance?

   Answer - If someone doesn't think they can do something, his/her performance will be impaired regardless of the actual ability.

7. Why are persons high in self-monitoring so effective in boundary-spanning positions? Can you think of jobs that they would not do very well?

   Answer - They are effective, because they are able to connect with other people and understand where they are at a given time in a given situation. They are willing to adapt to other's expectations, not simply push forward. High self-monitors would not do well as individual contributors with little contact with others or in situations where they would receive conflicting instructions from superiors.

8. If you suspect that someone with whom you are dealing is high in Machiavellianism, what steps should you take to protect yourself from this person?

   Answer - 1) Expose them to others. This neutralizes their ability to get ahead by lying and using dirty tricks. 2) Pay attention to what others do, not what they say. They will say one thing and do another. 3) Avoid situations where they have an edge, such as highly emotional ones or where others are unsure how to proceed.

9. Can you think of cultures that induce a low level of need for achievement among persons living in them? Are these cultures high or low in economic development?

    Answer - Students will be able to name various cultures based on their experience. Do some research and identify 2-3 examples you can share with the class. Be careful that the students don't fall into stereotyping; Mexicans are lazy, Nigerians are dishonest, etc. Focus the students on the cultural and the economic issues that contribute to the expectations about achievement.

10. Suppose that you're a morning person--you feel most alert and energetic early in the day. What steps can you take to make this characteristic a "plus" for your personal productivity?

    Answer - Students will have a variety of answers. For fun, have students identify themselves as morning or night people, put them into groups by type, all the night people together and all the morning people together, and see if you receive different strategies. Watch for students wanting to use stimulants, i.e., coffee, candy, etc., to overcome their low times.

11. As they get older, many people seem to become more "absentminded." Does this mean that their memory abilities are decreasing? If not, then what accounts for this change?

    Answer - Some memory ability does decline with age, especially short-term, which is the type of memory that contributes to "absentmindedness."

12. Is it ever appropriate to use personality tests as a hiring tool--a technique for deciding which persons to hire for a specific job? What are the potential dangers of using personality traits in this way?

    Answer - Conduct some personal research. In some cases the use of personality tests for selection is illegal. Companies may use them after a person has been selected, but they are often not considered valid selection tools. Also, the basic danger is that good people could be eliminated because the tools are misused. Personality tests can be one more way to reinforce stereotypes and discriminate.

Case in Point: Shooting for the Moon at Intel

You might give students the assignment of finding articles describing Intel. Grove has been on several periodical covers in 1996, and articles should be easy to find. This research will better enable students to answer the questions.

1. Do you think that Andy Grove's personality has contributed to Intel's amazing growth in recent years? If so, how?

    Answer - Students' answers will vary. It is apparent that Grove's constant drive to achieve has permeated the culture as Intel constantly strives to improve.

2. What about Intel's corporate culture, which is often described as being one of the most aggressive in the industry? Do you think Grove's personal traits helped to shape this culture?

    Answer - Students' answers will vary. Again, it seems obvious.

3. Suppose Grove retired next year. Would Intel change? Or would it remain largely on the course Andy Grove plotted for it?

    Answer - This is a question of the consequences of succession. Obviously it depends on who follows Grove and whether he retains any type of control. As students know, organizational cultures are hard to change, so they will probably argue things will continue.

4. How can seemingly incompatible traits such as vision and paranoia be combined within a single person? Or are these traits really as inconsistent as they seem?

Answer - The two aren't all that different as they both require imagination and the ability to collect and use seemingly unrelated information. Have students focus on Grove's particular definition of paranoia.

Skills Portfolios
Experiencing Organizational Behavior

Measuring Your Own Self-Monitoring
1. Photocopy the questions without the answers and hand out to the students.
2. Pass out the questions face down; have students write on the blank back of the questions if they would describe themselves as high, average, or low self-monitoring. Then have them turn the questions over and answer them.
2. Remind students the questions need only be mostly true or false to be selected.
3. Give everyone 10 minutes to take the "quiz."

Scoring
1. You can either read the correct answers or have the students refer to their texts.
2. On the board create three columns: 8-7   6-4   3 or below
3. Ask by show of hands who had a score that fit in each category.

Questions for Discussion
1. Begin by asking students if their "quiz" results matched their self-evaluation written on the back of the questions. Note on the board how many agreed or didn't agree with their results.
2. Focus on the pluses for both high and low self-monitoring people. Have students brainstorm the best jobs for each.
3. When answering Question #3, keep students from falling into stereotypes--Human Resources is a people job, engineering is a task-oriented job, etc.

Working in Groups
Machiavellanism in Action: The $10 Game
1. This is an excellent exercise. Try to form threesomes of strangers. If friends end up together, they can band together, throwing off the exercise, or damage a relationship when the division ends up not going their way.
2. Go out and buy play money, or use clipart and print off enough one dollar bills to use in the exercise. If you want to take high risk, get the students to each bring 4 one dollar bills to class the day you do this. The more real the money, the more real their responses.
3. Another variation is to appoint an observer for each group who records what happens in terms of the questions for discussion.

Questions for Discussion
1. Discuss as directed in the text.
2. Spend the most time on Question #4. Help the students develop real strategies for dealing with this type of people.

Chapter 5 - Motivation in Organizations

Learning Objectives

After reading this chapter, you should be able to

1. Define *motivation* and explain its importance in the field of organizational behavior
2. Describe *need hierarchy theory* and what it suggests about improving motivation in organizations.
3. Identify and explain the conditions through which *goalsetting* can be used to improve job performance.
4. Explain *equity theory* and describe some of the research designed to test its basic tenets.
5. Describe *expectancy theory* and how it may be applied in organizations.
6. Distinguish between *job enlargement* and *job enrichment* as techniques for motivating employees.
7. Describe the *job characteristics model* and its implications for redesigning jobs so as to enhance motivation.

Chapter Contents

		Page
Introduction		
I.	Motivation in Organizations: Its Basic Nature	142
II.	Need Theories of Motivation	144
	A. Need Hierarchy Theories	144
	B. Managerial Applications of Need Theories	147
III.	Goal-Setting Theory	149
	A. Locke and Latham's Goal-Setting Theory	150
	B. Managers' Guidelines for Setting Effective Performance Goals	151
IV.	Equity Theory	154
	A. Adams' Equity Theory	154
	B. Applying Equity Theory: Some Motivational Tips for Managers	157
V.	Expectancy Theory	159
	A. Basic Elements of Expectancy Theory	159
	B. Managerial Applications of Expectancy Theory	161
VI.	Job Design: Structuring Tasks for High Motivation	163
	A. Job Enlargement and Job Enrichment	163
	B. The Job Characteristics Model	166
	C. Techniques for Designing Jobs That Motivate: Some Managerial Guidelines	168
Summary and Review		170
Questions for Discussion		171
Case in Point		172
Skills Portfolio		173
Experiencing Organizational Behavior		173
Working in Groups		173

Chapter Outline

Instructor's Notes   Case Preview: Physician Sales and Service Company is a model of motivation, from the owner/founder's goal focus in everything he says and does, to tying employee compensation to company performance, to making business meetings fun. With 22% growth every year for the last five years and a goal of $1 billion in sales by 2001, PSS shows what proper motivation can do.

Introduction

1. Kelly at PSS tries to balance cash motivators with an atmosphere of fun in motivating employees.
2. OB's motivation strategies are based on science, where theory and practice are tied together.
3. This chapter will cover:
   a. the major approaches to motivation.
   - what each theory says.
   - what research there is to support it.

I. Motivation in Organizations: Its Basic Nature
   A. **Motivation: A Definition**
      1. the set of processes that arouse, direct, and maintain human behavior toward attaining some goal.
         - Arousal is the drive or energy behind action.
         - Direction is the choices people make.
         - Maintenance is the persistence of the behavior.
      2. Motivation and job performance are not synonyms.
      3. Motivation is multi-faceted, people have several different motives operating at one time.
         - See Figure 5-3. The Quest for Interesting Work.

II. Need Theories of Motivation
   A. **Need Hierarchy Theories**
      1. The best known of these is Maslow's Need Hierarchy Theory. He argued that people's needs were hierarchical, we satisfy one before we move on to the next, higher need. There are five basic needs in ascending order:
         - physiological - fundamental biological drives.
         - safety - security from physical and psychological harm.
         - social - friends, acceptance by others.
         - esteem - self-respect, approval by others.
         - self-actualization - self-fulfillment.
      2. There are several criticisms regarding Maslow's theory.
         - Research does not support the pure hierarchical approach.
         - There isn't much support for his specific assertions.
         - Research does not confirm the five categories.

3. Alderfer's ERG Theory is offered as a simpler alternative. There are only three levels, and they are not necessarily hierarchical. The three levels are:
   - existence which corresponds to Maslow's physiological and safety.
   - relatedness which corresponds to Maslow's social.
   - growth which corresponds to Maslow's esteem and self-actualization.
   - See Figure 5-4. Need Theories: A Comparison.

C. **Managerial Applications of Need Theories**
   1. If managers can help their employees reach the higher level of needs, they will be more satisfied and productive. Companies can do this by:
      - promoting healthy lifestyles.
      - providing financial security.
      - providing opportunities to socialize.
      - recognizing employee accomplishments.
   2. Rewarding needs to be done carefully.
      - The desired behaviors need to be rewarded.
      - The effects of rewards wear off over time.
      - The rewards need to be meaningful to the employees.

The Ethics Angle
Operation Frontline: Fighting the War Against Hunger
1. This is one example of how individual professionals can contribute to society at large.
2. Note for students that while it is a public project, it is still addressing the needs of people in order to motivate them to a more productive life.

III. Goal-Setting Theory
   A. **Locke and Latham's Goal-Setting Theory**
      1. The basic idea is that goals serve as motivators because they cause people to compare their present capacity to perform with that which is needed to succeed at the goals.
      2. They also believe that assigned goals become personal goals. People develop **goal commitment.**
      3. Finally, both self-efficacy and personal goals influence task performance.

   B. **Managers' Guidelines for Setting Effective Performance Goals**
      1. Managers have a number of activities for enhancing motivation.
      2. Assign specific goals. People perform at higher levels when asked to meet a specific high-performance goal.
      3. Assign difficult but acceptable performance goals. A goal must be difficult and specific in order to raise performance.
      4. Provide feedback concerning goal attainment.
         - See Figure 5-8. Feedback an Essential Aspect of Goal Setting.

The Quest for Quality
"Sabbaticals" Time Off Satisfies Many Needs Simultaneously
1. Sabbaticals were the domain of academe but are now being used to a good end by corporations.
2. Review the benefits of sabbaticals with students. The personal benefits are obvious. Help the students think about the bottom line benefits for the company.
   - They provide rest to employees.
   - They reward faithful service.
   - They provide the opportunity for personal growth.
3. Note that only the best employees, the high performers, are eligible for these programs.

Instructor's Notes

IV. Equity Theory
This is an individual-based theory that adds a social component-- the social comparisons people make, comparing themselves to others.

A. **Adams' Equity Theory**
   1. Proposes that people focus on two variables, outcomes and inputs.
      - Outcomes - what people get out of their jobs; pay, fringe benefits, prestige, etc.
      - Inputs - the contributions that people make to their jobs; time worked, effort expended, units produced, and qualifications brought.
   2. Based on these variables, individuals compare themselves to others, checking for equity. They see one of three states:
      - overpayment inequity.
      - underpayment inequity.
      - equitable payment.
      - See Figure 5-9 for the model. Equity Theory: An Overview.
   3. Based on their perception of equity or inequity, they respond by:
      - raising or lowering inputs.
      - raising or lowering outcomes.
   4. Sometimes individuals will not do what is necessary to address the inequity. In these cases they will change they way they think about the inequities.
   5. Equity theory is proving valid in both research and experience.
      - See Figure 5-10. Employee Theft: A Reaction to Underpayment.

B. **Applying Equity Theory: Some Motivational Tips for Managers**
   1. Avoid underpayment. A classic example of this is the two-tier wage system.
   2. Avoid overpayment. The benefits are temporary. People begin to think they deserve it. Other employees resent it.
   3. Present information about outcomes and inputs thoroughly

Instructor's Notes

and with social sensitivity.
V. Expectancy Theory
   A. **Basic Elements of Expectancy Theory**
       1. Expectancy theory is built on three core beliefs:
           * expectancy, the belief that effort results in performance.
           * instrumentality, the belief that performance will be rewarded.
           * valence, that the rewards are valued by the recipient.
       2. Performance needs to be instrumental in bringing rewards.
       3. Motivation comes from the interplay of the three beliefs.
           * See Figure 5-12. Expectancy Theory: An Overview.
       4. Finally, performance is also influenced by role perceptions, what people believe is expected of them on the job.
       5. Research supports the theory and the abundance of practical applications makes it popular with managers.

   B. **Managerial Applications of Expectancy Theory**
       1. Clarify people's expectancies that their effort will lead to performance.
       2. Administer the rewards that are positively valent to employees.
       3. Clearly link valued rewards and performance.
           * See Table 5-3. Ensuring Positively Valent Rewards.
       4. If properly administered these kinds of programs are highly effective and an organization needs to think about that before implementing them.
       5. Also, remember that rewards do not have to be monetary to be effective.

The Organization of the Future
Confronting the Challenge of Paying for Performance at the Top
1. While what executives get paid is not in the realm of what most business students think about, this case shows some of the significant issues in implementing pay-for-performance.
2. Have the students identify the issues; the concern that the people (executives) are not being paid according to their contribution, the move to longer term performance measurement, that pay-for-performance doesn't fit well with non-quantifiable jobs, etc.
3. Explore how Yoplait has overcome these and other problems.
4. Discuss why, with their problems, pay-for-performance programs are gaining in popularity?

Instructor's Notes

VI. Job Design: Structuring Tasks for High Motivation
    Job design is the idea that motivation can be increased by making the job more appealing to do. It is a movement away from scientific management's efficiency and back to treating people like people.
    A. **Job Enlargement and Job Enrichment**
        1. Job Enlargement - increasing the number of tasks at the same level. It is also known as horizontal job loading.
        2. Job Enrichment - increasing the number of higher level

tasks, or vertical job loading.

3. Both seem to improve job performance, but job enrichment seems to have a longer-lasting effect.
   - See Figure 5-13. Job Enlargement and Job Enrichment: A Comparison.
4. Job enrichment programs have met with some resistance due to:
   - the difficulty of implementation.
   - a lack of employee acceptance.
   - the need to tie compensation to enrichment to be completely effective.

B. **The Job Characteristics Model**
   1. Identifies how jobs can be designed to help people feel that they are doing meaningful and valuable work. There are five critical job dimensions:
      - skill variety - the degree to which the job requires different activities requiring different skills.
      - task identity - the extent to which a job requires completing a whole piece of work, from beginning to end.
      - task significance - is the degree of impact the job is believed to have on others.
      - autonomy - how free the employee is to plan, to schedule, and to carry out the work as desired.
      - feedback - does the job allow people to receive information about the effectiveness of their performance?
      - See Figure 5-14. The Job Characteristics Model: Its Basic Components.
   2. Skill variety, task identity, and task significance all contribute to a task's *experienced meaningfulness*.
   3. Autonomy contributes to people's feeling *personally responsible and accountable*.
   4. Feedback lets employees have *knowledge of the results of their work*.
   5. The model specifies that five critical psychological states affect feelings and outcomes.
      - Feelings of motivation.
      - The quality of work performed.
      - Satisfaction with work.
      - Absenteeism.
      - Turnover.
   6. This model is especially effective with people who are high in growth need strength.
   7. When the core job dimensions and their associated psychological reactions are in proper relationship, motivation is at its peak.

<u>Instructor's Notes</u>   8. The relationship can be assessed through a Job Diagnosis Survey (JDS). Based on the responses a formula can be set up to compute the motivating potential score or MPS.
- MPS = (Skill Variety + Task Identify + Task Significance)/3 x Autonomy x Feedback

9. While studies show positive gains in how employees feel about their jobs, when the MPS and enrichment strategies have been applied, there is no particular evidence showing improved performance will result.

You Be the Consultant

1. Have the students think through whether job enlargement or enrichment is a better strategy in this case. An argument can be made for either, but which is best? Have the students suggest specific changes they would make.

2. Try and find a few students who have worked in a factory and have them talk about their experience and what would have made it better for them. Many students have no concept of what manufacturing or factory work is like.

3. Again, with the rewards the justification is as important as the suggestion. Why do they want to do what they suggest? Have them discuss the downsides of their offered rewards.

<u>Instructor's Notes</u>   C. **Techniques for Designing Jobs that Motivate: Some Managerial Guidelines**

There are a number of ways a job can be designed with the job characteristics model. Table 5-4 and the list below offer some specific strategies.

1. Combine tasks - enhances skill variety and task identity.
2. Open feedback channels - enhances feedback.
3. Establish client relationships - enhances skill variety, autonomy and feedback.
4. Load jobs vertically - enhances autonomy.

Summary and Review

Questions For Discussion

1. <u>Based on Maslow's need hierarchy theory, what specific things can be done to enhance an employee's motivation?</u>

Answer - Managers should strive to help their employees reach the higher level of needs. This will make them more satisfied and productive. Companies can do this by; 1) promoting healthy lifestyles, 2) providing financial security, 3) providing opportunities to socialize, 4) recognize employee accomplishments. Rewarding needs to be done carefully. The desired behaviors need to be rewarded. The effects of rewards wear off over time. The rewards need to be meaningful to the employees.

2. <u>Why might setting goals be an effective way of motivating people on the job? What steps can be taken to ensure the effectiveness of goal setting in practice?</u>

    Answer - The basic idea is that goals serve as motivators because they cause people to compare their present capacity to perform with that which is needed to succeed at the goal. Assigned goals become personal goals. People develop goal commitment. Finally, both self-efficacy and personal goals influence task performance. Managers can ensure effectiveness in goal setting by; 1) Assigning specific goals. 2) Assigning difficult but acceptable performance goals. A goal must be difficult and specific in order to raise performance. 3) Providing feedback concerning goal attainment. See Figure 5-8. Feedback an Essential Aspect of Goal Setting.

3. <u>Suppose an employee feels underpaid relative to his/her co-workers. What conditions may have led to these feeling, and how might you expect such an individual to behave on the job?</u>

    Answer - If an employee feels that his/her outcomes (pay, fringe benefits, prestige, etc.) are greater than his/her inputs (time worked, effort expended, units produced, and qualifications brought). Based on these variables individuals compare themselves to others, checking for equity. If they perceive inequity they may respond by lowering inputs, or seeking a raise in their outcomes. Sometimes individuals will not do what is necessary to address the inequity. In these cases they will change they way they think about the inequities.

4. <u>Consider a poor performing employee who explains to his boss that he is trying very hard. According to expectancy theory, what factors would contribute to such effort? What additional factors, besides motivation, contribute to task performance?</u>

    Answer - The employee believes that his continuing effort will eventually result in performance and that performance will be rewarded. Also, he apparently values the rewards. Other factors that will contribute to task performance are the employee's role perceptions, clarity of expectancies, enhancing the valence, clearly linking the rewards to performance.

5. <u>According to the job characteristics model, what steps might be taken to enhance the motivation of someone performing a sales job?</u>

    Answer - Students should first think about what characteristics already exist in a sales job. Skill variety, autonomy, and feedback are part of all sales. They might recommend giving the sales person control over more of the entire process--task identity, or help the sales person understand how their sale fits into the overall picture--task significance.

6. <u>Explain the role that money plays as a motivator in all five theories of motivation presented in this chapter.</u>

    Answer - In Need Theory the money could meet anything from existence needs to growth in the sense of self-esteem. For Goal-Setting, a specific amount of money could be the goal sought. In Equity Theory money would be the measure for comparing oneself to others. In Expectancy Theory, money could be the valent reward. In Job Design money is less important. It could be a feedback tool.

Case In Point: Keeping Boeing Flying Higher and Higher

1. The goals that Mr. Shrontz set for Boeing were extremely difficult. What must have been done to make them so highly effective?

    Answer - Shrontz was able to arouse the employees and give them direction. He had to know what were attainable but difficult goals, so he had to know the business. Finally, the involvement of all the employees was crucial.

2. What do you think would have happened if Mr. Shrontz's goals were even more challenging?

    Answer - Students could choose two possible answers, 1) employees would have met them, 2) they would have been too high and employees would have given up. The important thing here is the justification the students offer.

3. In what ways did the new manufacturing methods keep the workers' jobs interesting enough so that they would work hard?

    Answer - The new processes probably increased task significance and feedback significantly. There may have been an increase in task identity for various work teams.

4. How do you think Boeing's computerized database system contributed to the engineers' motivation to do their jobs?

    Answer - The database was the pivotal technology that made all the changes possible.

Skills Portfolios

Experiencing Organizational Behavior

Assessing the Work Rewards You Personally Value

1. Follow the directions as offered in the text.
2. One variation that may help the students answer more accurately would be to have them picture the ideal job first, making some personal notes about it. Then think about the work-related rewards in that context.

Questions for Discussion

1. Handle the questions as they are offered.
2. With Question #2 have the students go back to the ten rewards and place a probability next to each representing their best estimates. 90% would be a strong certainty of attaining the reward. 10% would indicate a negligible possibility.
3. For Question #3 write the ten rewards on the board then poll the students as to which were their three highest rated rewards. Then lead the discussion.

Working in Groups

Does Goal Setting Really Work? Demonstrate It for Yourself

1. Follow the directions as written.

Questions for Discussion

1. Discuss the questions as they are offered.

Chapter 6 - Work-Related Attitudes: Feelings About Jobs, Organizations, and People

Learning Objectives
After reading this chapter, you should be able to:
1. Define *attitudes* and understand their basic components.
2. Identify and describe the major theories of *job satisfaction* and the techniques used to measure it.
3. Explain the major causes and consequences of job satisfaction.
4. Describe the major dimensions of *organizational commitment*, including its foci and bases.
5. Describe the major causes and consequences of organizational commitment.
6. Distinguish between *prejudice* and *discrimination*, and describe various types of prejudice in organizations.
7. Describe some of the steps being taken by organizations today to manage *diversity* in the workforce.

Chapter Contents   Page

Introduction

I.   Attitudes: What Are They   177

II.   Job Satisfaction: Attitudes Toward One's Job   178
    A. Are People Generally Satisfied with Their Jobs?   179
    B. Measuring Job Satisfaction: Assessing Reactions to Work   180
    C. Theories of Job Satisfaction   183
    D. Consequences of Job Dissatisfaction   185
    E. Promoting Job Satisfaction: Some Guidelines   188

III.   Organizational Commitment: Feelings of Attachment Toward Organizations   190
    A. Organizational Commitment: Its Basic Dimensions   190
    B. Consequences of Low Organizational Commitment   193
    C. Suggestions for Enhancing Organizational Commitment   193

IV.   Prejudice: Negative Attitudes Toward Others   196
    A. Diversity Versus Prejudice: Competing Organizational Realities   197
    B. Various "Groupisms": Manifestations of Prejudicial Attitudes in the Workplace   197
    C. Managing a Diverse Workforce: Current Practices   202

Summary and Review   206
Questions for Discussion   207
Case in Point   207
Skills Portfolio   208
    Experiencing Organizational Behavior   208
    Working in Groups   209

Chapter Outline

Instructor's Notes   Case Preview: Banking is not thought of as your cutting edge industry when it comes to human resource programs. But Canada's Bank of Montreal aggressively implemented a diversity program, with great success, focusing on women.

Introduction
1. Attitudes are important in our personal and work lives.
2. This chapter looks at the importance of job satisfaction, organizational commitment, and prejudices at work.

I. Attitudes: What are They?
   A. Attitudes have three major components to them:
      1. An evaluative component - how one feels.
      2. A cognitive component - how what you believe affects your attitude.
      3. A behavior component - Your predisposition to act based on your attitude.
         • See Figure 6-1. Three Basic Components of Attitude.
      4. **Attitude** is the relatively stable cluster of feelings, beliefs, and behavioral predispositions we possess about something.
         • Job satisfaction is the most basic of all work-related attitudes.

II. Job Satisfaction: Attitudes Toward One's Job
   A. **Are People Generally Satisfied with Their Jobs?**
      1. An international survey of three countries shows significant levels of satisfaction with work.
         • See Figure 6-2. Are People Satisfied with their Jobs: A Three Nation Comparison.
      2. Some key findings:
         • white-collar tend to be more satisfied than blue-collar.
         • older people are more satisfied than younger.
         • more experienced people are more satisfied than less experienced.
         • women and minorities tend to be less satisfied than men and majorities.

   B. **Measuring Job Satisfaction: Assessing Reactions to Work**
      1. Rating scales and questionnaires are the most commonly used tools for measuring job satisfaction. Three common types are:
         • Job Descriptive Index (JDI).
         • Minnesota Satisfaction Questionnaire (MSQ).
         • Pay Satisfaction Questionnaire (PSQ).

Instructor's Notes

2. Critical Incidents is a second procedure for assessing job satisfaction. Those involved relate:
    *   events that are especially satisfying at work.
    *   events that are especially dissatisfying at work.
3. Interviews and Confrontation Meetings, involve interviewing employees face-to-face. This permits in-depth exploration of employee answers.

The Quest for Quality

The "Happiness Index": Assessing Job Satisfaction at Wild Oats Market

1. The experience of Wild Oats Market shows the importance of employee perception that the owners pay attention to the feedback received in the survey.
2. Have students note the practical consequences of the happiness survey. Ask why employees cooperate with the survey. Help them see that the owners act as a consequence of the feedback.
3. Ask students what is unique about the Wild Oats experience with this job satisfaction survey.

Instructor's Notes

C. **Theories of Job Satisfaction**
    1. Herzberg's Two-Factor Theory
        *   Hygiene (maintenance) factors are associated with job dissatisfaction: quality of supervision, pay, company, policies, physical working conditions, relations with others, job security.
        *   Motivators are associated with job satisfaction: promotion opportunities, opportunities for personal growth, recognition, responsibility, achievement
        *   Help students see that most managers spend the majority of their time dealing with hygiene factors rather than motivators.
        *   See Figure 6-3. Herzberg's Two-Factor Theory.
    2. Locke's Value Theory
        *   Job satisfaction exists to the degree that outcomes received match outcomes desired.
        *   The larger the discrepancy between wants and haves in outcomes, the less satisfied an employee will be.
        *   See Figure 6-4. Job Satisfaction: The Result of Getting What We Want.

D. **Consequences of Job Dissatisfaction**
    1. When employees are dissatisfied, they reduce their exposure to the job by withdrawing in two key ways:
        *   absenteeism. Can cost $247-$534 per employee per unplanned absence.
        *   voluntary turnover. See Figure 6-5. Voluntary Turnover: A Model.
    2. Both of these are very costly. Economic conditions have the most effect on the search for alternative jobs.

3. While there is a positive link between job satisfaction and task performance, it is not strong nor direct because:
   - there is little room for large changes in performance in some jobs.
   - satisfaction and performance may not be directly linked.

E. **Promoting Job Satisfaction: Some Guidelines**
   1. Some suggestions of ways to promote job satisfaction:
      - Pay people fairly.
      - Improve the quality of supervision.
      - Decentralize the control of organizational power.
      - Match people to jobs that are congruent with their interests.

III. Organizational Commitment: Feelings of Attachment Toward Organizations
   A. **Organizational Commitment: Its Basic Dimensions**
      1. **Organizational commitment** is the extent to which an individual identifies and is involved with his/her organization and/or is unwilling to leave it.
      2. Employees may be committed to their co-workers, subordinates, supervisors, customers, union, or top management. These commitments break into two groups:
         - one's immediate work group and supervisor.
         - top management and the organization as a whole.
      3. There are four commitment profiles to these groups.
         - Uncommitted - low commitment to both groups.
         - Committed - high commitment to both groups.
         - Locally committed - high commitment to immediate work group and supervisor.
         - Globally committed - high commitment to top management and/or the organization.
         - See Table 6-2. Four Different Commitment Profiles.
      4. There are two approaches to understanding the bases or motives for commitment.
         - Side-bets orientation focuses on accumulated investments individuals will lose if they leave.
         - Goal-congruence orientation focuses on the extent to which people identifying with an organization have personal goals that are in keeping with those of the organization.
      5. Recent research points to three bases of organizational commitment:
         - continuance - related to side-bets. Refers to strength of people's tendency to continue to work for an organization because they can't afford not to.

- <u>affective</u> - related to goal-congruence. Refers to strength of people's tendency to continue to work for an organization because they agree with it.
- <u>normative</u> - related to the obligations one feels, the pressures from others to stay.
- See Figure 6-7. Organizational Commitment: Three Types.

B. **Consequences of Low Organizational Commitment**
1. High levels of absenteeism and voluntary turnover.
2. Unwillingness to share and make sacrifices.
3. Negative personal consequences.

C. **Suggestions for Enhancing Organizational Commitment**
1. Enrich jobs.
2. Align the interests of employees with those of the company.
3. Recruit and select newcomers whose values closely match those of the organization.
   - In this light pay careful attention to the organization's mission statement and communication of it. See Table 6-3. Mission Statements: Explicit Statements of Corporate Values.
   - Pay particular attention to the recruiting process.

IV. <u>Prejudice: Negative Attitudes toward Others</u>
1. A negative attitude we hold toward someone because of his/her membership in a particular group is a **prejudice**.
2. Behavior consistent with a prejudicial attitude is **discrimination**.
   - See Figure 6-9. Prejudice vs. Discrimination: A Key Distinction.
A. **Diversity versus Prejudice: Competing Organizational Realities**
1. While the U.S. has a highly diverse workforce, there is prejudice against some groups. This prejudice leads to a number of negative effects.
   - It is a source of serious friction or conflict.
   - It may have adverse effects on the careers of people who are the targets of such attitudes.
   - It has a devastating psychological impact on the targets of discrimination.

B. **Various "Groupisms": Manifestations of Prejudicial Attitudes in the Workplace**
1. Groupism is prejudice based on membership in certain groups, such as:
   - prejudice based on age.

Instructor's Notes

- prejudice based on physical condition.
- prejudice based on sexual orientation.
- prejudice based on race and national origin.
- prejudice against women.
- See Figure 6-12. Does Racial Discrimination Exist? It Depends on Who You Ask.

C. **Managing a Diverse Workplace: Current Practices**
1. Diversity management programs are efforts to celebrate diversity by creating supportive working environments.
2. There are two main types of diversity management programs:
   - <u>awareness-based</u>, designed to raise people's awareness of diversity issues in the workplace.
   - <u>skills-based</u>, designed to develop people's skills with respect to managing diversity.
   - See Figure 6-13. Diversity Management: Two Major Approaches to Training.
3. There are four main tools for developing skills in managing diversity.
   - cross-cultural understanding.
   - intercultural communication.
   - facilitation skills.
   - flexibility and adaptability.
4. There is evidence of long-range benefits to this training.
5. A number of major companies have successfully initiated diversity management programs.
6. Caution; there have been some problems.
   - They have sometimes reinforced stereotypes.
   - They have led to the perception of special treatment.
   - See Table 6-4. Potential Problems in Diversity Training.

The Ethics Angle
<u>Valuing Differences at DEC</u>
1. DEC has tried to enhance ethical behavior by supporting diversity.
2. Have students note what things DEC has done to capitalize on diversity. Do they think these are effective or not? What else would they suggest?

You Be the Consultant
1. The students' reasons for or against a diversity program are the key here. Manage this discussion carefully. The diversity of your own classroom will provide a rich resource pool of ideas, BUT also can have a few hidden "mines" if any students harbor hard feelings or prejudices.
2. As the students enumerate potential problems, don't let them use the problems as an excuse to do nothing. Students should differentiate between hassles and "deal-breakers" in terms of the seriousness of the potential problems.

Globalization and Diversity in Today's Organizations
Dealing with Diversity: Taking the Pulse of American Companies
1. Ask the students how diversity programs would help a company attract and retain talent. Do their comments apply to people not normally affected by diversity. Why or why not?
2. Note what companies are and are not doing regarding implementing diversity. Is it important that companies measure the effectiveness of their efforts? Why or Why not?

Summary and Review

Questions For Discussion

1. Someone tells you that people in general don't like their jobs. Would you agree or disagree with this statement? Why?

   Answer - Students should generally disagree. Some may agree because of their personal dissatisfaction with their work situations. However, an international survey of three countries shows significant levels of satisfaction with work. Refer students to Figure 6-2. Are People Satisfied with their Jobs: A Three Nation Comparison. Also, some key findings were: 1) white-collar tend to be more satisfied than blue-collar. 2) older people are more satisfied than younger. 3) more experienced people are more satisfied than less experienced. 4) women and minorities tend to be less satisfied than men and majorities. These findings may account for some difference of opinion regarding just how satisfied the workforce really is.

2. As a manager, you want to enhance job satisfaction among your subordinates. What steps might you take to accomplish this goal?

   Answer - The text suggest several ways to promote job satisfaction. 1) Pay people fairly. 2) Improve the quality of supervision. 3) Decentralize the control of organizational power. 4) Match people to jobs that are congruent with their interests. Ask students to give examples of what these four strategies might look like. Ask students to share other things that have enhanced their job satisfaction.

3. "Happy workers are productive workers." Do you agree or disagree? Why?

   Answer - This question can lead to some healthy, reality checking discussion. Students will naturally argue for agreement. However, the text points out that while there is a positive link between job satisfaction and task performance, it is not strong nor direct; because there is little room for large changes in performance in some jobs, and satisfaction, and performance may not be directly linked. This question will naturally lead into the discussion for Question #4.

4. Absenteeism and voluntary turnover are costly problems for many companies. What specific steps can be taken to reduce the incident of these forms of employee withdrawal?

   Answer - When employees are dissatisfied, they reduce their exposure to the job by withdrawing in two key ways: 1) absenteeism which can cost $247-$534 per employee per unplanned absence, and 2) voluntary turnover which is also costly. See Figure 6-5. Voluntary Turnover: A Model. Students can offer many suggestions from helping employees better match inputs and outcomes, to job enrichment strategies, to more equitable treatment and pay. Key here is the students understanding of the effort, cost, and effectiveness of the strategies they suggest.

5. <u>Suppose an employee is highly dissatisfied with his or her job and organization, but remains on the job and does not look for a new one. How would you explain this person's behavior?</u>

   Answer - Organizational commitment is complex. The worker might stay because he/she feels committed to his/her co-workers, subordinates, supervisors, customers, union, or top management. Students might discuss the approaches for understanding commitment; 1) Side-bets orientation which focuses on accumulated investments individuals will lose if they leave; and 2) Goal-congruence orientation which focuses on the extent to which people identifying with an organization have personal goals that are in keeping with those of the organization. Students should address the three bases of organizational commitment: 1) <u>Continuance</u> - related to side-bets. Refers to strength of people's tendency to continue to work for an organization because they can't afford not to; 2) <u>Affective</u> - related to goal-congruence. Refers to strength of people's tendency to continue to work for an organization because they agree with it; 3) <u>Normative</u> - related to the obligations one feels, the pressures from others to stay. Refer students to Figure 6-7. Organizational Commitment: Three Types.

6. <u>"Sexism and racism are a thing of the past."</u> <u>Do you agree or disagree? Why?</u>

   Answer - This is a potentially volatile question. Students will tend to speak from their experience not the text. Manage the process carefully because student responses will vary from cavalier to deep bitterness. Use the differences of opinion to demonstrate that at least the perception, and probably the reality, of these types of discriminations exist.

7. <u>What steps are today's organizations taking to manage diversity in their workforces? Give an example.</u>

   Answer - Diversity management programs fall into main types: <u>awareness-based</u>, designed to raise people's awareness of diversity issues in the workplace and <u>skills-based</u>, designed to develop people's skills with respect to managing diversity. Refer students to Figure 6-13. Diversity Management: Two Major Approaches to Training. Also note the four main tools for developing skills in managing diversity: 1) Cross-cultural understanding, 2) Intercultural communication, 3) Facilitation skills, and 4) Flexibility and adaptability.

Case in Point: Cultural Diversity at Exxon Chemical

1. <u>What impediments do you believe Exxon Chemical may face on its way to valuing the diversity of its employee base?</u>

   Answer - Students' answers will vary. Help students see prejudice is universal among people. Old opinions and ways of doing things die slowly, regardless of what people say.

2. <u>What steps can the company take to help overcome these barriers?</u>

   Answer - Students' answers will vary. Seek to draw out modeling by top management, policies that provide equal access to opportunities, and training as three key ways to address the issue.

3. In addition to the Choices program, what other measures could Exxon Chemical take to help encourage the acceptance of diversity within its workforce? Do you think it is realistic that such measure will actually help encourage diversity in a multinational workplace?

    Answer - The interesting thing here will be student responses. Again students will tend to speak from their experiences. Help them see that change is realistic if people commit to the change and top management leads the way. Again, manage the process, some students could have really deep hurts in this area, and the discussion could get heated.

4. Exxon Chemical officials are assuming that there are advantages to having a highly diverse workforce, if these can only be tapped. What, specifically, would you say these advantages are--especially in a large multinational organization like Exxon Chemical?

    Answer - Help students see that different perspectives bring different and often better solutions. Review group process and help them see that if some members of a group don't participate, the whole group suffers.

Skills Portfolios
Experiencing Organizational Behavior
Are You Committed to Your Job?
1. This may be a difficult exercise for some students who have only done part-time temporary work at this point in their lives. You can handle this in a couple of ways. First, have those students who have <u>not</u> held a full-time regular job imagine the job they want to get out of college. Have them write a paragraph description of that job and use it to think through the question. Second, have those students who have <u>not</u> held a full-time regular job choose their longest temporary job and answer in that context.
2. Consider having students reveal by a show of hands how many have held a full-time job more than six months. This will help you know where they are coming from in their answers.
3. Retyping the questions on a separate sheet without the answer key may help you to get more unadulterated answers.

Questions for Discussion
1. Discuss the questions as directed. Consider having students record what they think their levels and types of commitment are before they take the instrument. This will help in the discussion of Question #2.
2. Again remember, discussion may lag due to the lack of full-time regular employment among your students.
3. To lead the discussion for Question #4 you must either tabulate class responses on the board or place students into groups. Don't tabulate individual responses to the questions but rather who was strongest in continuance commitment, affective commitment, and normative commitment.

Working in Groups
Recognizing Differences in Cultural Values on the Job
1. This exercise can be conducted in either small groups or as a class.
2. A variation would be to assign students to defend and offer examples for one side or the other. Give the assignment ahead of time so that students can prepare examples.

Questions for Discussion

1. Manage this discussion carefully. A high risk but big payoff strategy would be to choose your most articulate male, woman, and minority person as primary respondents to the questions, either as a panel or individually. Their differences in perspective will be illuminating to the students. Don't try this unless you are very confident of your process skills.

2. Help students move beyond the easy answers and stereotypes in the discussion.

Chapter 7 - Career Development and Work Stress

Learning Objectives
After reading this chapter, you should be able to
1. Understand the concept of *socialization* and identify the stages through which it develops.
2. Explain what *mentors* are, what they do, and both the benefits and the costs of mentoring to mentors and their protégés.
3. Describe the process through which people choose their careers, and explain how the nature of careers have changed in recent years.
4. Explain how the careers of women and men may differ, including the impact of the *glass ceiling*, and differences in the way men and women react to the *midlife crisis*.
5. Define stress and distinguish between stress and strain.
6. Describe some of the major organizational and personal causes of stress, including conflict between work and family responsibilities.
7. Explain the concept of *burnout*, including its major causes and effects.
8. Describe the adverse effects of stress, and explain how individual difference factors play a role in such effects.
9. Describe both individual and organizational techniques for managing stress.

Chapter Contents

	Page
Introduction	
I. Organizational Socialization: The Process of Joining Up	214
A. The Nature of Organizational Socialization	214
II. Mentoring: One-on-One Socialization	216
A. What Do Mentors Do?	216
B. How Mentoring Relationships Form and Change	217
C. Gender, Race, and Mentoring	218
III. Careers: New Forms, New Strategies	219
A. Choosing a Job: Making Vocational Choices	220
B. Career Planning: Charting Your Future	221
C. Current Practice: Signs of Trouble In Your Career	225
D. Gender and Careers: Do Females and Males Have Different Experiences?	226
IV. Stress: Its Basic Nature	230
V. Stress: Its Major Causes	230
A. Work-Related Causes of Stress	230
B. Causes of Stress Outside Work	233
VI. Stress: Its Major Effects	235
A. Stress and Task Performance	235
B. Stress and Psychological Well-Being: Burnout	236
C. Stress and Health: The Silent Killer	237

VII. Managing Stress: Some Effective Techniques   238
    A. Personal Approaches to Stress Management   238
    B. Organization-Based Strategies for Managing Stress   240
Summary and Review   241
Questions for Discussion   243
Case in Point   243
Skills Portfolio   244
    Experiencing Organizational Behavior   244
    Working in Groups   244

Chapter Outline

Instructor's Notes

Case Preview: The case explains the personal stress experience of Sergio Zyman as he dealt with bringing Coca-Cola back from market decline.

Introduction

1. Beginning with Table 7-1--Bouncing Back From Failure, the chapter is setup to be a study in self-management--career and stress.
2. Some key terms:
   - Organizational socialization is the process by which new employees become full members of their organizations.
   - Mentoring helps younger and less experienced organizational members to receive help and guidance from older, more experienced members.
3. The chapter examines:
   - organizational socialization.
   - mentoring.
   - career and stress management.
   - the impact of gender on career.
   - stress and stress management.

I. Organizational Socialization: The Process of Joining Up
This is the process through which individuals are transformed from outsiders to participating, effective members of organizations. It's *learning the ropes*.

A. **The Nature of Organizational Socialization**
1. Getting in - Socialization actually begins before people accept a job. They acquire information about their company and new job.
   - Friends and relatives.
   - The organization via recruiters.
2. Entry shock is the negative reaction that sometimes occurs when new employees are surprised when entering an organization.

3. Realistic job previews, which provide accurate introductory information about the job, help minimize entry shock.
4. Breaking in is the second stage and begins when an individual assumes his/her responsibilities. This is when the individual learns the organization's culture.
   - Orientation programs help newcomers through this.
5. Settling in is when the individual attains full membership. This may be marked by a formal event. This is the most significant stage as it is the most permanent.

II. Mentoring: One-on-One Socialization
   When an experienced employee, the **mentor,** advises, counsels, etc., a new employee, the **protégé,** the protégé's career can receive a significant long-term boost.
   A. **What Do Mentors Do?**
      1. They perform a number of important functions.
         - Provide emotional support and confidence.
         - Nominate their protégé for promotion.
         - Provide opportunities to demonstrate competence.
         - Suggest strategies for reaching goals.
      2. Mentors do whatever is necessary to help their protégés' careers. As a consequence, there is competition for mentors among newcomers. Those who gain a mentor are often best at *impression management.*

   B. **How Mentoring Relationships Form and Change**
      1. The selection and matching process is complex. Both parties, mentor and protégé, are involved.
      2. Would-be protégés:
         - seek personal interactions with their boss.
         - negotiate terms of their relationship directly.
         - express a willingness to exceed expectations.
      3. Non-protégés tend to:
         - try to put themselves in a favorable light.
         - demonstrate conformity to formal role requirements.
      4. Mentor-protégé relationships have several distinct phases.
         - Initiation - lasts from six months to one year. This is the start of the relationship.
         - Cultivation - is the second phase, may last two to five years. The bond between mentor and protégé deepens, and the protégé makes rapid career progress.
         - Separation - in this third phase the protégé breaks free of his/her mentor. It may occur because the mentor feels unable to continue to help the protégé.
         - Redefinition - is the final stage, the bond becomes one of friendship and equality.
         - See Table 7-2. Mentorship Programs: What Some Companies Are Doing.

C. Gender, Race, and Mentoring

1. Various factors play a role in mentoring relationships.
   - People feel most comfortable around people like themselves.
   - Women tend to be less willing to be mentors than men.
   - Male managers are concerned about being mentors for women.

You Be the Consultant

1. Students' responses will vary; clearly a program could be established. Students should ask basic questions; such as, are there experienced women to be mentors, how to manage male mentors with female protégés, is top management committed to this or is it a gimmick to reduce turnover, etc.
2. Have students talk about the selection process and its stages. Ask students if they think the mentor or the protégé should have the final say in who is matched with whom.

III. Careers: New Forms, New Strategies

Significant changes are taking place in careers. A **career** is the evolving sequence of a person's work experience over time.

- In 1989, 70% of Stanford MBAs took corporate jobs. In 1994, less than 43% did.
- 43% of Northwestern Kellogg School rejected big company jobs.
- Many large companies have stopped coming to Harvard because so many students have stopped seeking corporate jobs.

A. Choosing a Job: Making Vocational Choices

1. People choose jobs partly based on who they are.
2. People also choose jobs because of the what they believe about the future.

B. Career Planning: Charting Your Future

1. Single-track careers are largely in the past.
2. Now and in the future people will take lateral moves, change careers, spend time as an independent contractor, etc. These changes have taken place because:
   - organizations have adopted a much flatter-internal structure.
   - businesses have focused more directly on their core businesses.
   - firms are using external contractors more often.

The Organization of the Future

The Hottest Careers of the Twenty-First Century

1. Ask them if they think these careers are the same ones that were hot 10 years ago, if they will be hot 10 years in the future.
2. Once the students have reviewed the various careers, help them see the importance of continuing education and training for career success. Help them see they need to continually grow personally.
3. See Table 7-3. Possible Winners in the Job Market of Tomorrow.

<u>Instructor's Notes</u>

3. In the future, careers will be a series of developmental opportunities, not a life-long job. The key question will become, "What will I learn from this?" not "How long will this job last?"

4. Four distinct career tracks are emerging:
   - The traditional straight, upward rise involving becoming an expert in corporate strategy.
   - Project managers who focus on the use of financial resources and human talent to accomplish projects
   - Resource provider who develops the talent and money for the project manager--example, Anderson Consulting.
   - Providing the talent, making it happen by their expertise or talent, content experts.
   - See Figure 7-3. Career Tracks In Today's Organizations.

5. Job rotation will become a regular part of any career. Currently this is happening to high-performers early in their career. Bottom-line don't hesitate to accept a job rotation opportunity.
   - See Figure 7-4. Job Rotation: A Plus for Many Careers.

C. **Current Practice: Signs of Trouble In Your Career**

1. There are warning signs that your career is stalled or in trouble. The following questions will help you see those signs.
   - Are you learning anything?
   - If your job were open, could you compete for it and get it?
   - Do you know what you are contributing?
   - What would you do if your career disappeared tomorrow?
   - Are you being exploited?
   - Are you worried about your job?

Globalization and Diversity in Today's Organizations
<u>Why the Japanese Won't Give Up Lifetime Employment</u>

1. Ask students if they agree or disagree with this perspective. There is significant evidence that the Japanese 1) don't practice this universally and 2) are in fact giving up lifetime employment.

2. Help the students think through the four reasons offered as to why lifetime employment will not go away. Do they find them valid or not?

D. **Gender and Careers: Do Females and Males Have Different Experiences?**

1. Men and women do have different experiences. Why they do is the result of a complex set of reasons, which can be somewhat summarized thus:

   - Increased training leads to managerial advancement, but seemingly more so for men than women.
   - Work experience and education are increasing in general, but again benefiting men more than women.
   - Having a spouse and dependents at home reduces women's work experience but increases men's.
   - Career encouragement is more closely tied to managerial advancement for women than for men.
   - Women do seem to have fewer developmental opportunities than men.

2. The percentage of women managers has almost tripled over the last 22 years. But the number of top women managers has only increased one and half times and remains at about 5% of all top managers.

   - Some argue the **glass ceiling** prevents women from reaching the top positions.

3. There is a debate over the existence of the glass ceiling.

   - The number of top jobs going to women is much smaller than would be predicted based on their proportion in the workplace.
   - It does not seem to be a conscious conspiracy by male managers, but may be influenced by the lower number of developmental opportunities for women.
   - Belief in the existence of the ceiling becomes a self-fulfilling prophecy.

4. Some women experience mid-life career crisis. A survey of successful career women showed:

   - More than 40% felt trapped.
   - Majority felt they didn't have enough personal time.
   - More than a third were bored.
   - 87% were contemplating a job change.
   - 56% reported a friend in therapy for personal problems.
   - See Figure 7-7. Women Executives Meet the Midlife Crisis.

5. These complaints peak at age 40-44. There is some debate as to why women are feeling this way. A big reason seems to be the personal cost.

6. More women are exploring entrepreneurship as a consequence.

7. Men are not opting out as much.

IV. Stress: Its Basic Nature
A. There are a number of **key terms** to understand before we can deal with stress.
1. <u>Stress</u> is pattern of emotional states and psychological reactions that occur in response to stressors.
2. <u>Stressors</u> are external demands, physical or psychological, encountered during the course of living.
3. <u>Strain</u> is the effect of stress resulting from the deviation from normal states of performance resulting from stressful events.
4. Key is that stress depends heavily on people's interpretation of what's happening to them. They will experience stress to the degree they perceive:
   - the situation as a threat.
   - they are unable to cope with it.

V. Stress: Its Major Causes
A. **Work-Related Causes of Stress**
1. Occupational demands make some jobs more stressful than others. Things like:
   - making decisions.
   - constant monitoring of devices or materials.
   - repeated exchange of information with others.
   - unpleasant physical conditions.
   - performing unstructured, rather than structured, tasks.
2. Conflict between work and nonwork, the competing demand causes stress.
   - The juggling of work and family responsibilities.
   - Role conflict, especially between work and family roles is extremely stressful.
3. Role ambiguity is experienced and leads to stress when people are uncertain about what actions to take to fulfill a job. This differs by country/culture.
   - It is low where there are large differences in power and status of management and subordinates and people act as groups rather than individually.
   - See Figure 7-8. Culture and Role Ambiguity.
4. Both overloading and underloading can create stress by:
   - <u>quantitative overload</u> - too much work, too little time.
   - <u>qualitative overload</u> - employee believes he/she lacks skill or ability to perform job.
5. Responsibility for others is a burden for some.
   - Managers must confront the human costs of organizational policies and decisions.
   - Manager must deal with frictions between people.

6. A lack of social support will increase stress. The following help:
    - friends help one feel more in contact.
    - friends may suggest helpful coping strategies.
    - friends can provide pleasant distractions.
7. Sexual harassment continues to be a problem in work settings.
    - Example offered of the Harris case.
    - Recent surveyed reported 31% of women and 7% of men had experienced harassment at work.

    The number of complaints has doubled since 1990.
    - But only 10% of women report it when harassed.
8. Unpleasant physical working conditions can also create stress.

B. Causes of Stress Outside Work
1. Stressful life events.
    - See Table 7-4. Stressful Life Events.
2. The hassles of daily life.
3. Total life stress.

VI. Stress: Its Major Effects
A. Stress and Task Performance
1. It has been assumed that mild stress improves performance. That is currently being questioned.
    - It can be distracting.
    - It is cumulative and builds to higher levels.
    - Even moderate stress can generate high arousal.
2. But, there are exceptions:
    - Highly skilled person sees a challenge, not a threat.
    - Individual differences exist.

B. Stress and Psychological Well-Being: Burnout
1. **Burnout** a syndrome that involves one or all of the following:
    - Physical Exhaustion; low energy, tiredness, headaches, nausea, poor sleep, changes in eating habits.
    - Emotional exhaustion, depression, feelings of helplessness, and feeling trapped in job.
    - Attitudinal exhaustion, cynicism about others, derogate selves, job, life in general, and report feelings of low personal accomplishment.
    - See Figure 7-9. Burnout: Its Major Components.
2. Burnout has several major causes.
    - Prolonged exposure to stress.
    - Job conditions.
    - Poor opportunities for promotion.

- Inflexible rules and procedures.
- Lack of consideration in leadership style of boss.
3. Burnout can be reversed by:
   - Reducing ongoing stress.
   - Gaining support from friends and co-workers.

C. **Stress and Health: The Silent Killer**
1. Burnout has a strong link to illness, especially degenerative and infectious diseases.
2. There are differences in individual resistance to stress, Type A's seem more susceptible to its harmful effects.
   - See Table 7-5. Personal Traits & Resistance to Stress.

VII. Managing Stress: Some Effective Techniques
A. **Personal Approaches to Stress Management**
1. Lifestyle management is one way to avoid the harmful effects of stress. Managing one's diet and exercising.
2. Physiological techniques, including meditation and relaxation training are highly effective.
3. Cognitive techniques, thinking yourself out of stress includes things as simple as reducing worrying by not *catastrophizing*.

B. **Organization-Based Strategies for Managing Stress**
1. Organizations can help as well by:
   - reducing family conflicts through family-supportive programs and policies.
   - offering stress management programs.
   - offering Employee Assistance Programs (EAPs).

The Ethics Angle
Fear as a Management Tool
1. Begin by discussing the appropriateness/inappropriateness of using fear as a management tool. Do students believe it is ever acceptable? Why or Why not?
2. Then analyze Semier's changes. Help students see that while fear was inappropriate, Semier may have gone too far the other way. Do not let students use the mistakes in this situation as excuses for not eliminating fear and giving employees more control over their jobs and their lives.

Summary and Review

Questions For Discussion

1. <u>What concrete steps can organizations take with respect to new hires to assure that they do not experience *entry shock* upon joining the company?</u>
    Answer - Entry shock is the negative reaction that sometimes occurs when new employees are surprised when entering an organization. This can be minimized by 1) realistic job previews, 2) orientation programs, 3) presenting the company as it really is in interviews, 4) mentoring programs, etc.

2. <u>How could you go about increasing the availability of mentors to women and minorities?</u>
    Answer - Answers will vary. Help students see the problem is more than a program problem but a perception and attitude problem, from women being more reluctant to mentor, to individual's preferring people "like themselves." Increasing awareness and appreciation of diversity, 'selling' women managers on the importance of the program, etc., are all partial solutions.

3. <u>What are the potential benefits of job rotation? Are there any potential drawbacks to such experience?</u>
    Answer - Answers will vary. Students should suggest they are developmental, keep work interesting, help reduce turnover, etc. Potential drawbacks, eventually you run out of jobs to rotate through, what if someone's not ready or capable for rotation but wants it, people lose the depth that comes from long time experience in the same position.

4. <u>Do you think it's true that women have more choice with respect to changing their careers at midlife than men? If so, why? If not, why?</u>
    Answer - The text presents evidence that there is a perception of women having more choices. Help students see that all adults have similar levels of responsibilities that require they work. Some students may try to use, "but women can get married." If they do, help them explore the prejudice that underlies that idea.

5. <u>Why are fewer and fewer graduates of MBA programs choosing to work for large corporations? Do you think their reluctance to accept such jobs is justified?</u>
    Answer - Answers will vary. Students need to see that these choices are trade-offs. It is not that corporations are bad and small companies are good but that they are different. Dissuade students of the idea that small companies don't have stress or aren't as demanding as larger companies.

6. <u>Why are the cognitive appraisals that individuals have about a given situation so important in determining the level of stress they experience in it?</u>
    Answer - Because the level of stress felt correspondences to what an individual thinks they are experiencing, what they think it means.

7. <u>Suppose that a female manager made several comments about the physique of a male subordinate. Would this constitute sexual harassment? Why?</u>
    Answer - Yes, but this will be a hot question. Monitor discussion carefully and don't let anyone get away with the comment, "Gee, I wish I could get some women to harass me." Help students see the issue is power related, not gender related, and it diminishes everyone involved.

8. Suppose you were faced with the task of choosing employees for a high-stress job. What personal characteristics would you seek in these individuals? What characteristics would you try to avoid?

    Answer - Actually, a bit of a trick question. While there are some personalities that seem to thrive on stress students should see there is no one best personality. It depends how well people cope, and you can't tell that until they are in the situation. Also, this question raises legal issues. Can a manager deny a job to someone simply because he/she doesn't think they can handle the stress? Answer - no.

9. What policies can organizations adopt to reduce stress among their employees resulting from family-work conflicts?

    Answer - Family-supportive policies. Have students name specific programs or policies, parental leave, child care, job-sharing, etc.

10. What steps can individuals take to effectively manage the stress to which they are exposed?

    Answer - Students should offer at least three broad strategies. 1) Lifestyle management is one way to avoid the harmful effects of stress. Managing one's diet and exercising.
    2) Physiological techniques, including meditation and relaxation training are highly effective. 3.) Cognitive techniques, thinking yourself out of stress, includes things as simple as reducing worrying by not catastrophizing.

Case in Point: Toyota, The Child Care Expert?

1. Do you think that running this subsidized child-care center is "good business" for Toyota? In other words, do the savings in terms of increased employee productivity justify the costs?

    Answer - Answers will vary, as there are no facts to substantiate a position. Make students justify their answers and move beyond global evaluations such as, "well of course," "no, of course not."

2. What about the childrens' health: Are the benefits of spending some time with their parents great enough to offset the costs of putting young children on a late night schedule?

    Answer - Answers will vary. Suggests an interesting research project.

3. How else could Toyota help employees to handle this problem?

    Answer - Students need to enumerate other family-supportive policies and programs that will help relieve family conflict.

4. Should Toyota consider the possibility of hiring for its night shifts only employees without young children? Would this be legal? Ethical?

    Answer - Help students see this is illegal discrimination, most likely to have an adverse impact on single women parents. Employers need to let employees make these choices.

Skills Portfolios
Experiencing Organizational Behavior
Developing a Personal Career Plan
1. Use exercise as directed.
2. This exercise will have its greatest value if the students turn in their plans and receive feedback. In large classes have one or two volunteers come up front and go through their plan for the whole class. The class gets some additional help but you do risk embarrassing an ill-prepared student. Avoid that problem by giving the students time to prepare and warn that you will choose one to discuss in class.

Working in Groups
The Worry Exercise
1. Use as directed in the text.

Questions for Discussion
1. As part of discussion, consider having a recorder from each group write the top three worries on the board <u>without</u> identifying who has those worries in their group.
2. Help students see that many people have the same worries they do.
3. Ask for coping strategies people have used successfully. Listen for those who suggest don't worry it doesn't do any good, party hardy, better living through chemistry, types of answers. Some students will say it to be cute but others may mean it.
4. Be careful to help students see that worry is normal, it can be managed, and that they are <u>not</u> bad or crazy because they worry.

Chapter 8 - Group Dynamics and Teamwork

Learning Objectives
After reading this chapter, you should be able to
1. Define what is meant by a *group*, and explain why it is not just a collection of people.
2. Identify different types of groups operating within organizations, and explain how they develop.
3. Describe the importance of *norms*, *roles*, *status*, and *cohesiveness* within organizations.
4. Explain how individual performance in groups is affected by the presence of others (*social facilitation*), the cultural diversity of group membership, and the number of others with whom one is working (*social loafing*).
5. Define what teams are and how they may be distinguished from groups in general.
6. Describe the various types of teams that exist in organizations and the steps that should be followed in creating them.
7. Understand the evidence regarding the effectiveness of teams in organizations.
8. Explain the factors responsible for the failure of some teams to operate as effectively as possible.
9. Identify things that can be done to build high-performance teams.

Chapter Contents   Page

Introduction
I. Groups at Work: Their Basic Nature   249
    A. What is a Group? A Working Definition   249
    B. Types of Groups   250
    C. Why Do People Join Groups?   252
    D. Stages in the Development of Groups   253
    E. The Structure of Work Groups   254

II. The Dynamics of Individual Performance in Groups   260
    A. Social Facilitation: Individual Performance in the Presence of Others   260
    B. Performance in Culturally Diverse Groups   265
    C. Social Loafing: "Free Riding" When Working with Others   266

III. Teams: Special Kinds of Groups   270
    A. Defining Teams and Distinguishing Them From Groups   270
    B. Types of Teams   272
    C. Managers' Guidelines for Creating Teams   274

IV. Effective Team Performance   276
    A. How Successful Are Teams? A Look at the Evidence   276
    B. Potential Obstacles to Success: Why Do Some Teams Fail?   278
    C. Building High-Performance Teams: Some Tips   280

Summary and Review   283
Questions for Discussion   283
Case in Point   284

Skills Portfolio   284
      Experiencing Organizational Behavior   284
      Working in Groups   285

Chapter Outline

Instructor's Notes

Case Preview: Teams in a printing company turned the company around, effecting its quality, its costs, its profits, and its employee morale and productivity.

Introduction

1. The importance and characteristics of group dynamics and teamwork are the foci of this chapter.
2. Some key terms:
   - **Group dynamics** focuses on the nature of groups--the variables governing their formation and development, their structure, their interrelationships with individuals, groups, and other organizations.
   - **Teamwork** refers to the practice of using teams, special kinds of groups, committed to some goal and sharing the leadership to attain it.
3. The chapter explains:
   - the history of the study of groups.
   - the nature of groups.
   - their stages of development.
   - the dynamics of their action.
   - specific types of groups.
   - high-performance teams.

I. Groups at Work: Their Basic Nature
    A. **What is a Group? A Working Definition**
        1. A group is a collection of two or more interacting individuals in a stable pattern of relationships, who share goals, and perceive themselves as a group.
        2. Group characteristics:
           - two or more people in social interaction.
           - stable structure.
           - members share common interests or goals.
           - individuals must perceive themselves as a group.
           - See Figure 8-1. A Group: Its Defining Characteristics.

    B. **Types of Groups**
        1. Formal and Informal Groups
           - Formal groups are created by an organization for an organizational purpose (command, task).
           - Informal groups develop naturally (interest, friendship).

- See Figure 8-2. Varieties of Groups in Organizations.

C. **Why Do People Join Groups?**
1. People join groups for a variety of reasons.
   - Mutual interest and goals.
   - Protection from other groups.
   - Social needs.
   - Self-esteem.
   - See Table 8-1. Why Do People Join Groups? Some Major Reasons.

D. **Stages in the Development of Groups**
1. Groups move through five stages of development. A group may be in any one stage for some time, they may not progress beyond a stage.
   - Forming - is a get acquainted stage, members are a bit confused as to how to work together.
   - Storming - conflict arises often over control and direction of the group.
   - Norming - groups enter this stage when leadership issues are resolved, relationships develop, interest builds in the group's goals.
   - Performing - the group is now working.
   - Adjourning - the task is completed, the group disbands.
   - See Figure 8-3. The Five Stages of Group Development.

E. **The Structure of Work Groups**
1. Group members tend to play specific roles.
   - **Role** - one's typical behavior is a social context.
   - **Role incumbent** is the member who holds the role.
   - **Role expectations** are simply what the member is expected to do.
   - **Role ambiguity** comes if there is confusion over expectations.
   - **Role differentiation** is the process by which members come to play the different roles in a group.
   - See Table 8-2. Some Roles Commonly Played By Group Members.
2. The implicit rules of a group are its **norms**. They are a shared way of viewing things. They can be **prescriptive,** dictating the behaviors that should be performed, or **proscriptive,** dictating the behaviors that should be avoided.

<u>Instructor's Notes</u>

3. Norms develop on the basis of:
    - precedents over time.
    - carryovers from other situations.
    - response to an explicit statement by a superior or co-worker.
    - critical events in the group's history.
    - See Table 8-3. Norms: How Do They Develop.

The Ethics Angle
<u>The Norm of Punishing Unethical Behavior at IBM</u>
1. This is an excellent example of the consequences of decisions.
2. Students will vary in their acceptance of IBM's policy. They will argue that "it depends." Help students see the bigger picture and to see that corporate policy must be fairly and equitably administrated.

<u>Instructor's Notes</u>

4. **Status** is the relative social position or rank given to groups or group members by others. Status comes in two basic forms:
    - Formal status (status symbols, perks).
    - Informal status (perception of others, skill based, etc.)
    - Higher status people tend to be more influential than lower status people.
5. **Cohesiveness** is the strength of group members' desires to remain a part of their groups. Cohesion is strengthened by:
    - the severity of the initiation to join the group.
    - a high external threat or competition.
    - the amount of time spent together.
    - the smallness of the group.
    - the group's history of success.
6. Group cohesion has some important consequences as well:
<u>Positive</u>
    - people enjoy membership.
    - members participate more fully.
    - they tend to be highly productive.
    - they experience low turnover.
<u>Negative</u>
    - groupthink arises when groups are too cohesive.
    - group commitment might hinder productivity.
    - groups may conspire to sabotage employers for the group's benefit.
    - See Fig. 8-6. Group Cohesiveness: Its Causes and Consequences.

Instructor's Notes   II. The Dynamics of Individual Performance in Groups

A. **Social Facilitation: Individual Performance in the Presence of Others**

1. When someone performs differently, either more effectively or less effectively, in the presence of others than when alone, they are experiencing **social facilitation**.

2. This phenomenon is explained by several psychological processes.
    - Individuals experience heightened emotional arousal.
    - Then when aroused they have a tendency to perform the most dominant response, what comes normally.
    - If the dominant response is appropriate, performance will be enhanced.
    - If the dominant response is inappropriate, as in a new situation, performance will be impaired.
    - See Figure 8-7. Social Facilitation: A Drive Theory Approach.
    - While there is a lot of research to support this theory, the "why" of it is still unclear.

3. Social facilitation may also result in evaluation apprehension, the fear of being evaluated or judged by another.

4. A third explanation is the distraction-conflict model which recognizes that the presence of others creates a conflict as to where attention is directed.

5. Computerized performance monitoring is a new influence on behavior. Research shows a significant decline in performance.
    - See Figure 8-8. Computer Monitoring: Evidence of Its Counterproductive Effects.

6. The implications are simple. Monitoring to keep performance high may actually reduce performance.

The Organization of the Future

Videoconferencing: Groups in Cyberspace

1. Have students discuss the benefits and costs to this type of mediated conferencing. The cost and time savings are clear. Are there any downsides to these technologies?
2. Kinkos, a national copying business, offers videoconferencing facilities for rent. Consider either taking the class or asking a small group to investigate the local Kinkos facilities and report their findings back to the whole class.

Instructor's Notes   B. **Performance in Culturally Diverse Groups**

1. Initially, culturally homogeneous groups outperform diverse groups.

2. Over time, the performance difference narrows until the diverse group outperforms the homogeneous group.

3. See Figure 8-9. Task Performance in Culturally Diverse Groups: An Experimental Demonstration.

C. **Social Loafing: "Free Riding" When Working with Others**
   1. **Additive tasks** are those in which each person's contributions are added together to another's. Unfortunately, as people work together, some in the group may ride on the efforts of others. This is **social loafing**.
      - See Figure 8-10. Social Loafing: Its General Form.
   2. Some explain social loafing through **social impact theory**, that the impact of any social force acting on a group is divided equally among its members. As a result, each member feels less than fully responsible for the outcome and puts in less effort.
   3. Another explanation is that the contributions of others makes each individual feel that his/her contribution is less important.
      - A contributing issue is that some members of a group may be more interested in getting something for themselves than getting something for the group.
      - A problem in individualistic cultures like the U.S., less so in a collectivistic culture like China.
      - See Figure 8-11. Social Loafing: Is It a Universal Phenomenon?
      - An experiment by Earley seems to confirm these patterns of behavior.
   4. Tips for eliminating social loafing.
      - Make each performer identifiable.
      - Make work tasks more important and interesting .
      - Reward individuals for contributing to their group's performance.
      - Use punishment threats.
   5. Social loafing is a potent force and productivity robber.

III. Teams: Social Kinds of Groups
   A. **Defining Teams and Distinguishing Them from Groups**
      1. A **team** is group whose members have complementary skills, are committed to a common purpose, and hold themselves mutually accountable.
      2. The key distinctives between a team and a group.
         - A team depends both on individual and collective work products.
         - A team focuses on individual and mutual accountability whereas a group is a pool of resources.
         - A team, like a group, shares common goals, but also shares a common commitment to purpose.
         - Groups are more responsive to management's demands, whereas a team focuses on and pursues a mission.
         - See Figure 8-12. Groups vs. Teams: A Comparison.
      3. Teams are special entities and may be self-managing or semiautonomous.

B. **Types of Teams**
1. Teams are classified according to four dimensions.
    - <u>Purpose or Mission</u> - are the basis of work teams or improvement teams.
    - <u>Time</u> - is the basis for temporary or specific projects versus permanent teams that are ongoing.
    - <u>Autonomy</u> - amounts to what degree the team makes its own decisions or has decisions made for it. Self-managed teams are the most autonomous of team structures.
    - <u>Authority</u> <u>Structure</u> - refers to the connection between the team and its various formal job responsibilities. Cross-functional teams are those with employees at the same level of responsibility but from very different functions within the organization. See Figure 8-14. The Boeing 777: A Product of Cross-Functional Teams.

C. **Managers' Guidelines for Creating Teams**
1. Designing work teams proceeds through four distinct stages, each with its own questions to be answered or decisions to be made.
2. Prework
    - Should a team be created?
    - Setting objectives.
    - Inventory of necessary skills.
    - What authority should a team have?
3. Creating performance conditions.
    - Proper working conditions.
    - Resources.
4. Forming and building the team.
    - Form boundaries.
    - Members must accept team's overall mission.
5. Provide ongoing assistance.
    - Teams guide themselves, but managers may be able to help shorten their learning by answering questions for them.
6. See Table 8-4. Stages of Team Creation: A Summary.

IV. <u>Effective Team Performance</u>
There are a number of reports of team effectiveness.
- Teams at Corning lowered defect rates to 9 parts per million.
- G.E.'s productivity in Salisbury, N.C. is two and one-half times higher than at other facilities.
- Westinghouse Furniture Systems saw a 74% increase in productivity over three years. Etc.

A. **How Successful Are Teams? A Look at the Evidence**
1. Measuring team success is difficult because of the different types of teams and their various responsibilities.

2. The most direct way to learn about their effectiveness is to survey the officials of the organizations using them wherever surveyed teams are highly regarded.
3. In-depth case studies provide different insights into teams' effectiveness.
4. Teams have been successful in manufacturing and service businesses.
    *   See Table 8-5. Teams in Organizations: Some Impressive Results.

B. **Potential Obstacles to Success: Why Do Some Teams Fail?**
    1. Despite success stories, some teams fail. Understanding why they fail will help organizations build winning teams.
        *   In some cases members were unwilling to cooperate with each other.
        *   Some teams lacked the support of management.
        *   Some managers were unwilling to relinquish control.
        *   Finally some teams fail because they won't cooperate with other teams.

Globalization and Diversity in Today's Organizations
Comparing Team Effectiveness in Japan, The United States, and Great Britain
1. What do the studies of the teams in three different countries tell us? Students should note that teams function differently but effectively in different countries.
2. Note for the students that these are not conclusive studies and the data needs to be carefully interpreted.
3. How could team effectiveness be measured quantitatively across cultures and tasks?

C. **Building High-Performance Teams: Some Tips.**
    1. Building high-performance teams takes planning and work: they don't just happen. There are a number of tips to help your efforts to be successful.
        *   Diversify team membership.
        *   Keep teams small in size.
        *   Select the right team members.
        *   Train, train, train.
        *   Clarify goals.
        *   Link individual rewards to team performance.
        *   Use appropriate performance measures.
        *   Encourage participation.
        *   Cultivate team spirit and social support.
        *   Foster communication and cooperation.
        *   Emphasize the urgency of the team's task.
        *   Clarify the rules of behavior.
        *   Regularly confront teams with new facts.
        *   Acknowledge and reward vital contributions to the team.

Summary and Review

Questions For Discussion

1. What is the difference between a collection of individuals and a group? Why is a "group" of people waiting in line to see a movie not really a group?

   Answer - Students should answer by providing the description of a group. A **group** is a collection of two or more interacting individuals in a stable pattern of relationships who share goals and perceive themselves as a group. A **group** has the following characteristics: two or more people in social interaction, stable structure, members share common interests or goals, individuals must perceive themselves as a group. See Figure 8-1. A Group: Its Defining Characteristics.

2. Identify the stages of group development described in the text and apply them to any group to which you belong. Do all the stages apply?

   Answer - The students' applications will vary but they should mention all the stages, explaining which do not apply and why. Groups move through five stages of development. A group may be in any one stage for some time. They may not progress beyond a stage. Forming - is a get acquainted stage, members are a bit confused as how to work together. Storming - conflict arises often over control and direction of the group. Norming - groups enter this stage when leadership issues are resolved, relationships develop, interest builds in the groups goals. Performing - the group is now working. Adjourning - the task is completed, the group disbands. See Figure 8-3. The Five Stages of Group Development.

3. Give examples demonstrating how norms, roles, and status operate within any groups to which you may belong.

   Answer - Students' answers will vary, but the answers should demonstrate the basic definitions of these terms. Group members tend to play specific roles. **Role** - one's typical behavior is a social context. Role incumbent is the member who holds the role. Role expectations are simply what the member is expected to do. Role ambiguity comes if there is confusion over expectations. Role differentiation is the process by which members come to play the different roles in a group. See Table 8-2. Some Roles Commonly Played By Group Members. The implicit rules of a group are its **norms**. They are a shared way of viewing things. They can be prescriptive, dictating the behaviors that should be performed, or proscriptive, dictating the behaviors that should be avoided. See Table 8-3. Norms: How Do They Develop. **Status** is the relative social position or rank given to groups or group members by others. Status comes in two basic forms: Formal status (status symbols, perks) and informal status (perception of others, skill based, etc.)

4. Imagine that you are about to go on stage to give a solo piano recital. How would the phenomenon of social facilitation account for your performance?

    Answer - Consider changing the question to giving a presentation in class. More students can identify with that. Most students will talk about how it will lessen performance, be sure to have someone talk about how it can or would heighten their performance. What follows is the explanation of the behavior; help the students apply it specifically to this situation. When someone performs differently, either more effectively or less effectively in the presence of others than when alone, they are experiencing **social facilitation**. This phenomenon is explained by several psychological processes. 1) Individuals experience heightened emotional arousal. 2) Then when aroused they have a tendency to perform the most dominant response, what comes normally. 3) If the dominant response is appropriate, performance will be enhanced. 4) If the dominant response is inappropriate, as in a new situation, performance will be impaired. See Figure 8-7. Social Facilitation: A Drive Theory Approach.

5. Describe an incident of social loafing in which you have been involved (e.g., a class project). What might be done to overcome this effect?

    Answer - Students' answers will vary, but it may be factory work, writing a group paper, or completing some group project, but look for the key elements. **Additive** tasks are those in which each person's contributions are added together with another's. See Figure 8-10. Social Loafing: Its General Form. **Social impact theory**, the impact of any social force acting on a group is divided equally among its members. As a result, each member feels less than fully responsible for the outcome and puts in less effort. Another explanation is that the contributions of others makes each individual feel that his/her contribution is less important. Have the students apply the Tips for eliminating social loafing to their specific situation, not all will apply. 1) Make each performer identifiable. 2) Make work tasks more important and interesting. 3) Reward individuals for contributing to their group's performance. 4) Use punishment threats.

6. What makes a team a special form of group? Is a baseball team really a team or is it just a group?

    Answer - A team is group whose members have complementary skills, are committed to a common purpose, and hold themselves mutually accountable. The key distinctives between a team and a group: 1) A team depends both on individual and collective work products. 2) A team focuses on individual and mutual accountability--whereas a group is a pool of resources. 3) A team, like a group, shares common goals, but also shares a common commitment to purpose. 4) Groups are more responsive to management's demands, whereas a team focuses on and pursues a mission. See Figure 8-12. Groups vs. Teams: A Comparison. Help students see that a baseball team could be either, that only an effective baseball team--committed, building on each other's accomplishments, and goal focused--is really a team.

7. Based on the evidence regarding the effectiveness of teams, would you say that the popularity of teams today is well founded?

    Answer - Encourage students to argue both sides of the question. The research seems to clearly support the use of teams, but teams don't work in all situations. Help the students think through in what types of situations teams would be effective. Bring in the reasons teams fail to help them.

8. Suppose you were to compose a work team in your organization. What potential pitfalls would you expect? What might you be able to do to help make that team perform at high levels?

    Answer - Students could create a laundry list. Have students create a more specific work situation in their answer. Then help them to think about which pitfalls and corrections would really work in the situation they imagine. Some teams fail because: 1) In some cases members were unwilling to cooperate with each other. 2) Some teams lacked the support of management. 3) Some managers were unwilling to relinquish control;.4) Finally some teams fail because they won't cooperate with other teams. Building high-performance tips: a) Diversify team membership. b) Keep teams small in size. c) Select the right team members. d) Train them. e) Clarify goals. f) Link individual rewards to team performance. g) Use appropriate performance measures. h) Encourage participation. i) Cultivate team spirit and social support. j) Foster communication and cooperation. k) Emphasize the urgency of the team's task. l) Clarify the rules of behavior. m) Regularly confront teams with new facts. n) Acknowledge and reward vital contributions to the team.

Case in Point: XEL: The Little Telecommunications Company That Could

1. What measures could XEL take to help make its teams as effective as possible?

    Answer - Students will see that these teams are working well and that some corrections have been made. Help them see that further refinements can still be made. The teams are too large at 12 each. They've seen the need to select the right team members. There needs to be some changes in training, especially new members. Have they linked individual rewards to team performance? What performance measures are they using? Are they cultivating team spirit and social support. Etc.

2. What problems are XEL's teams likely to face and how can they be overcome?

    Answer - Some of the problems have already surfaced: abuse of system, inability to accept new members, etc. Students should see that the task focus may keep them from cooperating with other teams.

Skills Portfolios
Experiencing Organizational Behavior
Why Do You Join Groups?

1. Have the students write down at the end of the statement "I joined this group because . . .," the group they joined.
2. Review the scoring that 1 is low and 5 is high. Someone will get it backwards if you don't.
3. Ask students what types of groups they joined and list the categories on the board,;this will help you focus the discussion. You may see a pattern, i.e., most people joined a social group, a religious group, or a sport-related group, etc. You can also use this to help the students analyze the differences in what was important to them.

Scoring
1. Score as directed.

Questions for Discussion
1. Before discussing, put the four categories on the board: seek satisfaction of mutual interests, achieve security, social needs, and feel good about yourself.

2. When you discuss Question #1, record how many people had each as their most important need. This will give you a sense of where the class is coming from. There may not be a pattern, but if there is, it will be helpful to know it.
3. Use the categories of groups you recorded earlier to facilitate your discussion of Question #2.

<u>Working in Groups</u>
Demonstrating the Social Loafing Effect
1. Explain the directions carefully. Additive tasks can become confusing if someone in the process is not clear on what they are doing.
2. Monitor each group to make sure the process is proceeding as directed, but don't interfere with any social loafing you may observe. Just correct the process if its being done incorrectly.
3. Otherwise conduct as directed.

Questions for Discussion
1. Handle the discussion carefully. Students could fall into accusation rather than observation, especially if students have worked as a team on some other project.
2. Discuss as directed in the exercise.
3. You could have the class conduct this exercise as an experiment in other classes. You could offer incentives, bonus points on an exam for the top two teams, and see the effect.

Chapter 9 - Interpersonal Communication in Organizations

Learning Objectives

After reading this chapter, you should be able to
1. Describe the process of *communication* and its role in organizations.
2. Identify various forms of verbal media used in organizations and explain which ones are most appropriate for communicating messages of different types.
3. Explain how style of dress and the use of time and space are used to communicate nonverbally in organizations.
4. Describe various types of individual differences with respect to how people communicate with each other.
5. Distinguish between formal and informal *communication networks* and explain the influence of each on organizational communication.
6. Describe how the formal structure of an organization influences the nature of communication that occurs within it.
7. Identify and describe measures that can be taken by both individuals and organizations to improve effectiveness of organizational communication.

Chapter Contents   Page

Introduction
I.   Communication: Its Basic Nature   289
    A. Communication: A Working Definition and Description of the Process   289
    B. The Fundamental Role of Communication in Organizations   291

II.   Verbal Communication: The Written and Spoken Word   292
    A. Varieties of Verbal Media in Organizations   292
    B. Uses of Oral and Written Communications: Matching the Medium to the Message 294
    C. When Words Go High-Tech: Special Issues of Electronic Media   295

III.   Nonverbal Communication: Speaking Without Words   297
    A. Style of Dress: Communicating by Appearance   298
    B. Time: The Waiting Game   298
    C. The Use of Space: What Does it Say About You?   299

IV.   Individual Differences in Communication   300
    A. Personal Communication Style   300
    B. Sex Differences in Communication: Do Women and Men Communicate Differently? 302
    C. Cross-Cultural Differences in Communication   303

V.   Communication Networks: Formal Channels of Information in Groups   303
    A. Varieties of Formal Communication Networks   304
    B. Formal Communication Networks and Task Performance   306

VI.   Informal Communication Networks: Behind the Organizational Chart   307
       A. Organizations' Hidden Pathways   307
       B. The Grapevine and the Rumor Mill   308

VII.   Organizational Structures: Directing the Flow of Messages   311
       A. Organizational Structure: Its Impact on Communication   311
       B. Communicating Up, Down, and Across the Organizational Chart   312
       C. Communication Inside vs. Outside the Organization   315

VII.   Overcoming Communication Barriers: Techniques for Enhancing
       the Flow of Information   316
       A. Keep Language Simple: Eschew Obfuscation   317
       B. Be an Active, Attentive Listener   317
       C. Gauge the Flow of Information: Avoiding Overload   320
       D. Obtain Feedback: Opening Upward Channels of Communication   321

Summary and Review   323
Questions for Discussion   324
Case in Point   325
Skills Portfolio   326
       Experiencing Organizational Behavior   326
       Working in Groups   327

Chapter Outline

Instructor's Notes

Case Preview: The case of Childress Buick/Kia shows how management can open the lines of communication and create a better working climate. In response to feedback that most employees didn't know what was going on with the business, the company initiated a number of communication efforts. As a consequence, turnover is down, profits are up, and customer satisfaction is up.

Introduction
1. There is evidence that employees' overall performance is strongly related to their competence as communicators.
2. Organizational communication is what holds an organization together.
3. The chapter covers:
   • the process of communication and its role in organizations.
   • the major influences on communication at various levels.
   • various elements of communication; formal vs. informal, structure, shape, direction, and flow of communication, etc.
   • the barriers to effective communication.

<u>Instructor's Notes</u>

I. <u>Communication: Its Basic Nature</u>

   A. **Communication: A Working Definition and Description of the Process**

      1. **Communication** is the process by which someone transmits information to someone else. This process has a number of elements to it.
- Encoding - the translating of the idea into a form to be communicated.
- Channel - the pathway or means of communicating.
- Decoding - the converting of the message by the receiver into the sender's original ideas.
- Feedback - the transmission of a new message back to the sender.
- Noise - an interference or distortion of the message in the process.
- See Figure 9-2. The Communication Process.

   B. **The Fundamental Role of Communication in Organizations**

      1. Communication has a number of roles and purposes.
- <u>Direct</u> action - one person telling another what to do.
- <u>Coordinated</u> action - getting people to work together, coordinate their activities.
- <u>Interpersonal</u> action - the building of relationships and trust.

II. <u>Verbal Communication: The Written and Spoken Word</u>

   A. **Varieties of Verbal Media in Organizations**

      1. Verbal media may take the form of:
- face-to-face conversations.
- non-face-to-face interactive, such as a telephone.
- static, one way communication, such as memos, letters, newsletters, handbooks.
- See Figure 9-3. A Continuum of Verbal Communication Media.

      2. Two key forms of written or static media are:
- <u>newsletters</u> - regularly published internal documents describing information of interest to employees. See Figure 9-4. Staying on the Road to Communication.
- <u>employee handbooks</u> - describe all the employees' basic information about the company. Their major purposes are:
  - to explain key points of company policies.
  - to clarify expectations.
  - to express the company's philosophy.
  - to aid in the socialization of employees.

B. Uses of Oral and Written Communication: Matching the Medium to the Message

1. Communication is most effective when it uses multiple channels, such as both oral and written messages.
   - Oral messages gain attention.
   - Written messages are more permanent and may be referred to in the future.
2. Two-way communication is used more often than one-way.
3. It is important to match the medium to the message to enhance effectiveness.
   - Oral better for ambiguous messages.
   - Written better for clear messages.
   - See Figure 9-5. Oral vs. Written Communication: Preference for Media Depends on the Message.
4. Media-sensitive managers were more effective than media-insensitive managers.

C. When Words Go High-Tech: Special Issues of Electronic Media

1. Video Display Terminals (VDTs) for computers have changed the way information is handled in most companies' offices. But they can lead to isolation as employees interact with a screen rather than a person.
2. Electronic Mail (e-mail) is a system whereby people use personal computer terminals to send and receive messages from each other. It's rapid and highly efficient, but depth and richness is lost.
   - There have been problems with e-mail, largely around misuse and abuse of privacy.
   - Electronic Communications Privacy Act only covers messages over phone lines or public networks. It does not cover private facilities such as company networks.
   - Employers can and do read employee e-mail.
   - See Table 9-1. A Model Employee Communication Policy.
3. Voice Messaging allows the sending of verbal messages, adding back the depth and richness lost in e-mail.
   - It is a very useful tool, as over 3/4s of business calls are nonimmediate.
   - Some companies believe it is saving them significant amounts of money.

III. Nonverbal Communication: Speaking Without Words

A. Style of Dress: Communicating by Appearance

1. Some feel what we wear communicates a great deal about our competence.
2. The key is appropriate dress, which varies with the circumstance.

B. **Time: The Waiting Game**
   1. People with special skills in high demand can make others wait.
   2. People communicate their status through making others wait for them.

C. **The Use of Space: What Does it Say about You?**
   1. The large office and office furniture convey status.
   2. Where someone sits at a table in a meeting conveys status.
      - See Figure 9-5. The Head of the Table: A Good Location for Communication.

IV. Individual Differences in Communication
   A. **Personal Communication Style**
      1. This simply means the consistent ways people go about communicating with others.
      2. There are six major communication styles.
         - The Noble - tend to say what's on their minds without filtering it.
         - The Socratic - carefully discuss things before making decisions. They enjoy arguing their points.
         - The Reflective - concerned with interpersonal aspects of communication, they are careful in what they say, concerned with offending others.
         - The Magistrate - mixes Noble and Socratic by telling what they think but in great detail.
         - The Candidate - mixes Socratic and Reflective. They are warm and supportive while being analytical and chatty.
         - The Senator - has both the Noble and the Reflective styles, unmixed. They move between them.
         - See Figure 9-7. Personal Communication Styles: A Summary.
      3. Everyone has the potential to use any of the styles.

   B. **Sex Differences in Communication: Do Women and Men Communicate Differently?**
      1. Men and women do communicate differently.
         - Men emphasize and reinforce their status.
         - Women downplay status.
         - Men use "I," try to exude confidence and see questions as a sign of weakness.
         - Women use "we," focus on the social connections, downplay their confidence, and aren't afraid to ask questions.

2. As a result, men and women respond differently to problems.
    *   Women listen and lend support.
    *   Men take control.
    *   Women ask questions.
    *   Men confront.
3. The consequences are simple, people in power tend to reward people whose linguistic styles match their own.

C. **Cross-Cultural Differences in Communication**
    1. The challenge in cross-cultural communication is that the same word can mean different things in different languages.
    2. Tone or inflection is often as important as the spoken word.

You Be the Consultant
1. Students can look at this in a number of ways, gender communication differences, communication style differences, or cross-cultural differences. Students can draw from several different areas of the text, including the Globalization and Diversity in Today's Organizations sidebar.
2. There are various solutions, but education and training would be primary even at the individual level. Unless individuals are aware and given skills, behavior and organizational climate can't change.
3. Students responses will vary. Help students be realistic. Organizational change is very hard, firing or punishing people isn't helpful either. Help students draw up a strategic plan for long-term, permanent change.

Globalization and Diversity in Today's Organizations
Breaking Down the Barriers to Cross-Cultural Communication
1. These suggestions are quite straightforward. Ask students for experiences they've had with international students and/or when traveling abroad.
2. While these suggestions apply to cross-cultural communication, ask students if they've ever been subject to evaluation, jumping to conclusions, someone not being able to see their perspective. How did they feel? How effective was their communication in those situations.
3. To help students grasp taking another's perspective, pick two students--one male, one female--and have them role play a situation you give them. After about 5-7 minutes, make them switch roles, have the male take the female role, and vice versa. Let them role play another 5-7 minutes, then ask them how they felt in the opposite role.

V. Communication Networks: Formal Channels of Information in Groups
    A. **Varieties of Formal Communication Networks**
        1. Organizations have a variety of communication networks in them. They are classified by their degree of centralization.
            *   Centralized networks pass information through a central person and may take the form of a "Y," a wheel, or a chain.
            *   Decentralized networks have free information flows, where all members have equal access to information, such as with a circle or comcon.

B. **Formal Communication Networks and Task Performance**
  1. Centralized networks are best with simple tasks.
  2. Decentralized networks are best with complex tasks.
  3. The greater the amount of information a person deals with, the greater the degree of **saturation,** which is why centralized networks work best with only simple tasks.
  4. Decentralization improves complex task performance because it reduces the problem of any one individual reaching saturation.
      - See Figure 9-10. Comparing the Performance of Centralized and Decentralized Communication Networks.
      - Most people prefer involvement and therefore prefer decentralized communication networks.
  5. Formal communication networks play an important role in organizations. However:
      - the longer groups are in operation, the less the limitations of various communication networks affect them.
      - the differences between communication networks fade with time.
      - they operate in conjunction with informal communication networks.

VI. <u>Informal Communication Networks: Behind the Organizational Chart</u>
   Informal communication happens when information is shared without any formally imposed obligations or restrictions.
   A. **Organizations' Hidden Pathways**
     1. People transmit information to those with whom they come in contact.
     2. As people spend more time with some rather than others, this type of communication is limited.
     3. Turnover seems to be tied to informal communication. Turnover seems to be related to those who communicate with each other a great deal. Someone knows someone who left for another job and uses that information and relationship to move themselves.
     4. Communication networks are composed of people on different levels of an organization.
         - See Figure 9-11. Informal Communication Networks: A Predictor of Turnover Patterns.

   B. **The Grapevine and the Rumor Mill**
     1. The **grapevine** is the pathway of unofficial, informal information. It is far faster than formal communication. The grapevine improves cohesion and social interaction.

2. One study found that 82% of information through a grapevine can be accurate. The problem is figuring out what portion of the message is inaccurate.
3. **Rumors** do go through the grapevine, messages with no basis in fact. Rumors contribute to grapevine's poor reputation.
4. Organizations can be injured by rumors.
5. It is difficult to combat rumors, they tend to have a life of their own.
   - Direct refutation may help, or it may feed the rumor.
   - Directing attention away from the rumor, focusing attention on the positive things people do know, may help.

VII. <u>Organizational Structures: Directing the Flow of Messages</u>
   A. **Organizational Structure: Its Impact on Communication**
      1. An **organizational chart** describes an organization's structure.
         - It lays out the formal lines of communication and responsibilities.
         - It shows lines of authority.
         - See Figure 9-12. The Organizational Chart: An Organization's Formal Communication Network.
      2. The better employees are integrated into an organization's formal structure, the better they adapt to new technologies.

   B. **Communicating Up, Down, and across the Organizational Chart**
      1. **Downward communication** consists of instructions, directions, and orders--messages to subordinates.
         - Subordinates do not always perceive messages accurately. Often there is a significant discrepancy.
         - It flows from one level to the next lower level.
         - The most effective techniques are small groups and organizational publications targeted to specific groups.

The Quest for Quality
<u>"You're Fired!": Tips for Humanely Communicating the Bad News</u>
1. Most people have a hard time separating the person from the event. If they get fired, they are bad people, and that is not true. Help students see that these steps help separate the two issues.
2. You might ask who has been fired and if they'd share their experience. This is somewhat high risk. While everyone gets "fired" sometime during his/her life, he/she generally doesn't like to talk about it. But if you can discuss an actual case it will help bring these steps into the real world.
3. Remind students that firing someone humanely may also have a practical effect of lessening the possibility of an unjust termination suit and help the fired person get on with his/her life and career more quickly.

---

2. **Upward communication** flows from subordinate to superior. It is not the reverse of downward, the issue here is status.
   - It happens less often than downward.
   - It tends to suffer from serious inaccuracies as people put the best picture forward they can.
   - It tends to omit bad news.
3. **Horizontal communication** flows laterally and is largely coordinating communication. It involves people with similar status.

C. **Communication Inside vs. Outside the Organization**
   1. See Figure 9-13. Internal vs. External Communications Is There a Difference?
   2. The message is different depending on where it is aimed.

VIII. <u>Overcoming Communication Barriers: Techniques for Enhancing the Flow of Information</u>
   A. **Keep Language Simple: Eschew Obfuscation**
      1. Using needlessly formal language may impose a serious barrier to communication.
      2. **Jargon** is the specialized language of a group, organization, or profession. Unfortunately, those outside of those entities may not understand the jargon.
      3. **KISS** - Keep it short and simple. People better understand messages that don't overwhelm them.
         - See Table 9-2. A Memo That Leaves You Scratching Your Head: "What Did He Say?"

   B. **Be an Active, Attentive Listener**
      1. Listening is an active process.
      2. A good listener:
         - asks questions and puts the speaker's ideas into his/her head.
         - avoids jumping to conclusions or evaluating.
         - ensures understanding before answering.
      2. The HURIER model of communication is composed of:
         - hearing.
         - understanding.
         - remembering.
         - interpreting.
         - evaluating.
         - responding.
         - See Fig. 9-14. The HURIER Model: Components of Effective Listening.
      3. When you invite people to talk you implicitly agree to listen to them. Listening not only helps you hear but makes those speaking feel good about you and the interaction.

C. **Gauge the Flow of Information: Avoiding Overload**
    1. Because people are busy and have many competing demands placed on them, they can experience **overload**, getting bogged down in more information than they can handle.
        - Some organizations use **gatekeepers** to control the flow of information.
        - Overload can be avoided through **queuing,** the lining up of incoming information so it can be handled in an orderly manner.
        - See Figure 9-15. Overload: A Problem That Can Be Solved.
    2. When systems overload, the organization experiences **distortion** and **omission**, i.e., the changing or omitting of information when it is passed from one organization to another.
    3. Strategies for avoiding distortion and omission are **redundancy**, the transmitting of the messages again, and **verification,** making sure the message has been received accurately.

D. **Obtain Feedback: Opening Upward Channels of Communication**
    1. Companies can facilitate communication with employees by various means.
        - Suggestions systems.
        - Corporate hotlines.
        - Brown bag and skip-level meetings.
        - Employee surveys.
    2. See Table 9-3. Obtaining Employee Feedback: Some Useful Techniques.

The Ethics Angle

Sears Installs the "Ethics Assist" Line

1. Ask students what they think of the telephone number Sears chose for their hotline. Do they think it will help or hinder their purpose for the hotline.
2. Students should pick up that the ethics effort is one of several co-ordinate initiatives.
3. Ask students what else Sears could be doing from a communications perspective to help improve the ethical environment in the company.

Summary and Review

Questions For Discussion

1. Using an example of an everyday communication in an organization (e.g., a supervisor asking her assistant for the month's production schedule), describe how the communication process operates (e.g., how information is encoded, etc.).

   Answer - Answers will vary by student. Students may confuse encoding with transmission and decoding with receiving. Students need to include noise or interference and feedback to have a complete model.

2. Imagine that you are a district manager attempting to explain a new corporate policy to a group of plant managers. Should this be accomplished using written or spoken communication, or both? Explain your decision.

   Answer - Students can argue for either, but a combination is the best. Note that oral messages gain attention. Written messages are more permanent and may be referred to in the future. Therefore an initial message should be oral, followed by written documentation. Two-way communication is used more often than one-way. It is important to match the medium to the message to enhance effectiveness. Oral is better for ambiguous messages. Written is better for clear messages. See Figure 9-5. Oral vs. Written Communication: Preference for Media Depends on the Message.

3. Suppose you're interviewing for a job. Describe how the way you dress and the interviewer's use of time and space can influence what you communicate to each other.

   Answer - The key with dress is appropriateness. It can communicate personal confidence and fit with the organization. The interviewer might make the student wait to convey status. The space and physical surroundings chosen for the interview also conveys status and importance.

4. You have a new co-worker with whom you find yourself having difficulty communicating. Explain the kinds of individual differences that might be responsible for this and what can be done to overcome them.

   Answer - There are six major communication styles. The Noble - tend to say what's on their minds without filtering it. The Socratic - carefully discuss things before making decisions. They enjoy arguing their points. The Reflective - concerned with interpersonal aspects of communication, they are careful in what they say, concerned with offending others. The Magistrate - mixes Noble and Socratic by telling what they think but in great detail. The Candidate - mixes Socratic and Reflective. They are warm and supportive while being analytical and chatty. The Senator - has both the Noble and the Reflective styles, unmixed. They move between them. See Figure 9-7. Personal Communication Styles: A Summary. Students will suggest a variety of strategies, but at their root should be accommodation to the other styles--communicating the content and the way the other style is most comfortable with.

5. Your company is being victimized by a totally untrue rumor about a pending merger. What steps would you recommend taking to put the story to an end? Explain.

   Answer - Answers will vary. Key is that students understand that their very strategies used to manage the rumor may feed it. Direct refutation may help, or it may feed the rumor. Directing attention away from the rumor, focusing attention on the positive things people do know, may help.

6. In Shakespeare's Hamlet, Polonius said, "Give every man thine ear, but few thy voice." Discuss the implications of this advice for being an active listener. What other suggestions should be followed for enhancing the effectiveness of listening?

    Answer - Listening is an active process. A good listener: 1) Asks questions and puts the speaker's ideas into his/her head. 2) Avoids jumping to conclusions or evaluating. 3) Ensures understanding before answering. Also, see Fig. 9-14. The HURIER Model: Components of Effective Listening.

Case in Point: Communicating All the Right Messages at General Motors

1. In what ways did the things that Mr. Actis did at General Motors help overcome the company's communication problems? What made his actions so effective?

    Answer - The fact that he used several different channels and modes to communicate. He worked at adapting the message to the audience. He modeled active listening and seeking feedback.

2. To what extent do you think that the success enjoyed by General Motors might be generalized to other types of organizations? Would these same actions work just as well in a service business, for example?

    Answer - Yes. If students don't think they would, have them explain why. Obviously a smaller company would not, could not, be as extensive in its choice of modes of communication.

3. What additional steps could be taken to enhance communication in this General Motors plant?

    Answer - Students' answers will vary. Cross-cultural efforts, considering gender communication issues, etc., are additional ways to enhance communication.

Skills Portfolios

Experiencing Organizational Behavior

Assessing Your Personal Communication Style

1. Ask students to not look at the scoring instructions until they've taken the instrument. Consider photocopying this page without the scoring information and passing out copies. If students read how to score the instrument before they complete it, it will skew their scores.
2. Emphasize that students should answer the questions based on what they do, not what they think they should do. Students might have a close friend fill out the instrument on them and compare the results.
3. Emphasize that this is a neutral test, no style is better than another.
4. Have students record what they think their style is.

Scoring

1. Score as directed.
2. Emphasize that there is no one best style.

Questions for Discussion

1. If students had a friend complete the instrument on them, have students compare the results.
2. Discuss other questions as directed.
3. Consider grouping students by style and have them create two lists, things they can do to be more effective with other styles, and what other styles can do to be more effective with them.

<u>Working in Groups</u>
Sharpening Your Listening Skills
1. Conduct as directed.
2. One variation is to have a third person, an observer join each pair and note effective behaviors and give feedback to the communicators.

Questions for Discussion
1. Discuss as directed.

Chapter 10 - Decision Making in Organizations

Learning Objectives
After reading this chapter, you should be able to
1. Identify the steps in the *analytical model* of decision making.
2. Describe reliable individual and cultural differences with respect to *decision styles*.
3. Distinguish between *programmed* vs. *nonprogrammed* decisions, *certain* vs. *uncertain* decisions, and *top-down* vs. *empowered* decisions.
4. Understand the *rational-economic* model, the *administrative* model, and *image theory* as approaches to decision making.
5. Describe how *framing effects*, the reliance on *heuristics*, a bias toward *implicit favorites*, and the *escalation of commitment* phenomenon dictate against high-quality decisions in organizations.
6. Compare the advantages and disadvantages of using groups and individuals to make decisions in organizations.
7. Describe the conditions under which groups make better decisions than individuals and the conditions under which individuals make better decisions than groups.
8. Explain *groupthink*, and how it may be a barrier to effective group decisions.
9. Describe techniques that can be used to improve the quality of group decisions (e.g., *individual decision training*, the *Delphi technique*, the *nominal group* techniques, and the *stepladder* technique).

Chapter Contents

	Page
Introduction	
I. Organizational Decision Making: Its Basic Nature	331
A. A General, Analytical Model of Decision Making	332
B. Decision Style: Individual Differences in Decision Making	334
C. Cultural Differences in Decision Making	335
II. The Broad Spectrum of Decisions in Organizations	336
A. Programmed versus Nonprogrammed Decisions	336
B. Certain versus Uncertain Decisions	337
C. Top-Down versus Empowered Decisions	339
III. Individual Decisions: How Are They Made?	339
A. The Rational-Economic Model: In Search of the Ideal Decision	340
B. The Administrative Model: Exploring the Limits of Human Rationality	341
C. Image-Theory: An Intuitive Approach to Decision Making	341
IV. Individual Decisions: What Makes Them Imperfect?	343
A. Framing Effects	343
B. Reliance on Heuristics	344
C. Bias Toward Implicit Favorites	345
D. Escalation of Commitment: Throwing Good Money After Bad	346
E. Organizational Barriers to Effective Decisions	348

V. Group Decisions: Do Too Many Cooks Spoil the Broth?   348
    A. The Pros and Cons of Group Decisions   349
    B. When Are Groups Superior to Individuals?   350
    C. When Are Individuals Superior to Groups?   352

VI. Groupthink: Too Much Cohesiveness Can Be a Dangerous Thing   353
    A. The Nature of Groupthink   353
    B. Strategies for Avoiding Groupthink   354

VII. Improving the Effectiveness of Group Decisions: Some Techniques   355
    A. Training Individuals to Improve Group Performance   355
    B. The Delphi Technique: Decisions by Expert Consensus   358
    C. The Nominal Group Technique: A Structured Group Meeting   359
    D. The Stepladder Technique: Systematically Incorporating New Members 361

Summary and Review   362
Questions for Discussion   363
Case in Point   363
Skills Portfolio   364
    Experiencing Organizational Behavior   364
    Working in Groups   365

Chapter Outline

Instructor's Notes	Case Preview: The case outlines a series of successful decisions of Jack Tate and his partner, Linda Robertson, and the incredible success that followed each. How he made the decisions is <u>not</u> explained, just the results.

Introduction
1. Decision making is something everyone does every day. It is the process of making choices from among several alternatives.
3. The chapter:
    - reviews the general nature of the decision-making process and the variety of decisions made in organizations.
    - will examine theories, research, and practical techniques.
    - begins with individual decision making, the factors that adversely affect their decisions, and techniques for improving the quality of those decisions.
    - then moves into group decisions: what makes those decisions imperfect, and techniques for improving the quality of those decisions.
    - See Figure 10-1. Decision Making: A Basic Organizational Process.

I.   Organizational Decision Making: Its Basic Nature

    A. **A General, Analytical Model of Decision Making**

       1.   Traditionally, decision making has been conceptualized as a series of analytical steps.

       2.   This process highlighted formulation of the problem and implementation of the final decision.

       3.   Decision making does not necessarily follow a neat pattern like this eight step model, but the model is still useful.

- Problem Identification - deciding what the problem actually is so you treat the problem and not a symptom.

- Define the objectives to be met in solving the problem - what is it that you want the solution to accomplish?

- Make a Predecision - deciding how to make the decision.

- Alternative Generation - creating several possible solutions so you can choose the best.

- Evaluate Alternative Solutions - using objective criteria to decide which solution is best.

- Make a Choice - deciding.

- Implement the Chosen Alternative - acting on the decision.

- Follow-up - monitoring the effectiveness of the decisions as they are put into action.

- See Figure 10-2. The Traditional, Analytical Model of Decision Making.

    B. **Decision Style: Individual Differences in Decision Making**

       1.   There are important differences among people with respect to how they make decisions--their **decision style**.

       2.   Research shows there are four major decision styles.

- The directive style prefers simple, clear solutions. Decisions are made rapidly because they use little information and do not consider many alternatives. They rely on existing rules and use their status.

- The analytical style considers more complex problems based on ambiguous information. Using as much data as possible, they carefully consider their decision, enjoying the process, and seeking the best quality decision.

- The conceptual style is more socially oriented, considers broader alternatives, and seeks creative solutions. This person is strongly future-oriented and enjoys initiating new ideas.

- The behavioral style is deeply concerned about the organization and personal development of others. Highly supportive of others, open to suggestions, seeking to help, they rely on meetings for decisions.

3. These differences in style can lead to conflict and difficulty in making decisions. But research suggests:
   - some people, such as corporate presidents, do not have a dominant style and can move between styles.
   - different groups are dominated by a style in making a particular decision.
   - some stereotypes, i.e., military leaders as authoritarian, do not fit their decision style, in this case conceptual.
   - that people do use very different approaches to solving the same problem.

C. **Cultural Differences in Decision Making**
   1. While people do seem to follow the same basic steps of decision-making across the world, the *way* decisions are made vary.
   2. In some countries--Thailand, Indonesia, or Malaysia, for example--interruptions in supplies/raw materials would be accepted as fate and not problem solved as it would be in the U.S.
   3. In the U.S., Canada, or Western Europe, people would see it as a problem for which as solution must be found and a decision made.
   4. The who, how, and how much time of decision making is reflected in the various characteristics of the country's culture.

II. The Broad Spectrum of Decisions in Organizations
   A. **Programmed versus Nonprogrammed Decisions**
      1. The question is, is the decision made repeatedly with a pre-established set of alternatives, or is each situation unique?
         - Programmed decisions are routine, made by lower-level personnel, and rely on predetermined courses of action.
         - Nonprogrammed decisions are for situations with no ready-made solution, each situation is unique.
         - Strategic decisions are a type of nonprogrammed decision made by coalitions of high-level executives.
      2. When distinguishing between the two types of questions, one should ask three questions:
         - What type of tasks are involved?
         - How much reliance is there on organizational policies?
         - Who makes the decisions?
      3. See Table 10-1. Programmed and Nonprogrammed Decisions: A Comparison.

   B. **Certain versus Uncertain Decisions**
      1. These types of decisions are concerned with the degree of risk involved.

2. Risk is measured in terms of the probability of achieving the desired outcome. It takes into consideration:
    *   objective probabilities based on concrete verifiable data.
    *   subjective probabilities based on personal beliefs and hunches.
    *   See Figure 10-4. The Riskiness of a Decision: A Summary.
3. Uncertainty may be reduced by:
    *   establishing linkages with other organizations.
    *   gathering more information.

C. **Top-Down versus Empowered Decisions**
    1. When subordinates gather information, give it to superiors who make decisions without involving subordinates, you have top-down decision making.
    2. Empowered decision making allows subordinates to make decisions without first checking with superiors.
        *   See Figure 10-5. Volvo Employees Make Empowered Decisions.

The Ethics Angle
Maguire Group Empowers Employees to Decide Own Ethics Policy
1. Ask students if this was an appropriate decision to delegate to employees. Why did Maguire Group let the employees decide?
2. Why do you think the ethics code reduced ethical violations?

III. Individual Decisions: How Are They Made?
A. **The Rational-Economic Model: In Search of the Ideal Decision**
    1. The model uses decisions to maximize the attainment of goals by systematically searching for the optimum solution to a problem.
    2. It follows the same steps as the traditional model but calls for an evaluation of all alternative courses of action.
    3. The model is **normative** in that it describes the ideal process and assumes that people have access to complete and perfect information.
    4. Unfortunately, this model does not describe real human behavior.

B. **The Administrative Model: Exploring the Limits of Human Rationality**
    1. The model recognizes that decision makers may have a limited view of the problems confronting them, and the alternatives and solutions are also limited.
    2. Solutions are considered as they come forward.

3. The first alternative that meets criteria is selected and the process stops.
4. This is a **satisficing decision** one that meets criteria but may not be the optimum decision.
5. Also, it recognizes **bounded rationality**, that people often lack the cognitive skills to formulate and solve highly complex problems.
6. As a descriptive approach, it more accurately represents what people actually do than the rational-economic model.

C. **Image-Theory: An Intuitive Approach to Decision Making**
1. Selecting the best alternative is not always a major concern, people often consider their personal standards in the process.
2. **Image theory** sees decisions as more intuitive than analytically rational. It focuses on decisions about courses of action, or changing current courses of action, and it is a two-step process:
    *   A compatibility test - comparing a course of action to the various images one holds regarding personal principles, current goals, and plans for the future.
    *   A profitability test - to what extent the various alternatives best fit their values, goals, and plans.
3. These two decisions are made within a decision frame - a consideration of meaning of the information in the context of the decision.
    *   See Figure 10-6. Image Theory: A Summary and Example.
4. According to this theory:
    *   we learn from the past.
    *   are guided by that learning.
    *   the process is very rapid and simple.
    *   we do not ponder or reflect, but rather make decisions with minimal cognitive processing.
5. The administrative model and image theory represent how people actually decide. The rational-economic approach is a theoretical model.

IV. Individual Decisions: What Makes Them Imperfect?
A. **Framing Effects**
1. Framing is how the problem is presented to the individuals involved. It affects how decisions are made.
2. This happens because people perceive equivalent situations presented differently as not equivalent.
    *   It is a cognitive bias.
    *   See Figure 10-7. Framing Effects: An Empirical Demonstration.

B. **Reliance on Heuristics**
1. Another cognitive bias.
2. When faced with complex decisions, people use simple rules of thumb to guide them--**heuristics**.
3. There are two types of heuristics:
   - available heuristic - which represents people making decisions based on the information readily available to them.
   - representativeness heuristic - refers to the tendency to perceive people stereotypically if they appear to be typical representatives of the category.
4. Heuristics do not always interfere with the quality of the decision made.
5. The heuristics are common to daily life. One simply needs to guard against stereotypes.

C. **Bias Toward Implicit Favorites**
1. People tend to have a preferred alternative, their **implicit favorite,** in mind in almost every decision.
2. Other options are considered as **confirmation candidates,** information used to confirm the preferred alternative even if the data from the confirmation candidate must be distorted.
3. People tend to make their decisions very early in the process.

D. **Escalation of Commitment: Throwing Good Money After Bad**
1. It is the tendency for people to continue to support previously unsuccessful courses of action because of the 'sunk costs' already invested.
2. People do this because of the need for **self-justification,** saving face, in order to protect their beliefs about themselves as rational, competent decision makers by affirming that their original decision was right all along.
2. Escalation of commitment is less likely when:
   - available funds for making further investments are limited.
   - the threat of failure is obvious.
   - they are able to diffuse responsibility for earlier failing actions.
   - the total amount invested exceeds the amount expected to be gained.
   - See Figure 10-8. Escalation of Commitment: An Overview.

Instructor's Notes

E. **Organizational Barriers to Effective Decisions**
1. There are a number of factors that interfere with the capacity to make decisions.
   - Time constraints.
   - Political "Face-Saving" Pressure.
   - Bounded Discretion (Moral and Ethical Constraints).

The Quest for Quality
Guidelines for Making Ethical Decisions
1. Discuss with students the connection between quality and ethicality for an organization. Is there one? If so, how?
2. Select an ethical situation from the Wall Street Journal, or another business publication, and walk the students through it, using the six questions offered in this quest for quality. There have been several prominent incidents over the last two years of automobile manufacturers cutting corners, of financial service companies cutting corners, etc., to choose from. Recently, an Internet service was caught rounding charges up when billing.
3. Help students find an example from campus life and apply these questions to it. Perhaps they saw/know of another student who cheated on a major project or exam, but they did nothing about it.

Instructor's Notes

V. Group Decisions: Do Too Many Cooks Spoil the Broth?
A. **The Pros and Cons of Group Decisions**
1. Advantages
   - Pooling of resources.
   - Specialization of labor.
   - Greater acceptance of the decision by those affected.
2. Disadvantages
   - Waste more time.
   - Group conflict.
   - Intimidation by group leaders.
3. See Figure 10-9. Group Decision Making: Advantages and Disadvantages.

B. **When Are Groups Superior to Individuals?**
1. When the group is heterogeneous and members have complimentary skills.
2. When expertise is used properly: the experts are listened to.
3. When the task is complex.
4. When team members can correct and assist each other.
5. Figure 10-10. Group vs. Individual Performance on a Complex Task: Empirical Evidence.

C. **When Are Individuals Superior to Groups?**
1. Individuals are superior to groups when working with poorly structured tasks or creative tasks.
   - See Figure 10-11: Group Decisions: When Are They Superior to Individual Decisions?

2. **Brainstorming** is a creative problem-solving technique for groups. There are four main rules:
   - Avoid criticism of ideas as they are offered.
   - Share all suggestions, even far-out ones.
   - Offer as many comments as possible.
   - Build on others' ideas.
3. Individuals tend to be more productive than groups. Groups tend to slow the process.

VI. <u>Groupthink: Too Much Cohesiveness Can Be a Dangerous Thing</u>
   A. **The Nature of Groupthink**
      1. This phenomenon has been studied in the context of some classic bad decisions:
         - Bay of Pigs.
         - Vietnam War.
         - Shuttle Challenger launch.
      2. Groupthink strikes all types of organizations, including corporations. The business setbacks of Lockheed and Chrysler are key examples.
      3. See Figure 10-12. Groupthink: An Overview.

   B. **Strategies for Avoiding Groupthink**
      1. A few proven techniques for avoiding groupthink.
         - Promote open inquires.
         - Use subgroups.
         - Admit shortcomings.
         - Hold second-chance meetings.

VII. <u>Improving the Effectiveness of Group Decisions: Some Techniques</u>
   A. **Training Individuals to Improve Group Performance**
      1. Group performance can be significantly improved through the selection and training for four common problems.
         - <u>Hypervigilance</u> - for quick solutions and guarding against them.
         - <u>Unconflicted adherence</u> - deals with sticking to the first idea and not considering either the problems with it or other ideas. This can be managed by: 1) thinking about difficulties of the idea, 2) thinking about other ideas, 3) considering special/unique issues of the problem.
         - <u>Unconflicted change</u> - changing the mind too quickly without due consideration. This can be managed by asking themselves about: 1) the risks/problems of adopting the solution, 2) the good points of the first idea, 3) the relative strengths/weaknesses of both ideas.
         - <u>Defensive avoidance</u> - an avoidance of the task at hand. Can be managed by: 1) avoiding procrastination, 2) avoiding disowning responsibility, 3) not ignoring corrective information.

The Organization of the Future
Decisions at 30,000 Feet: Technology Helps Pilots Avoid Fatal Errors.
1. Discuss with students the possible consequences of poor decisions for a company, for their employees.
2. In what other situations can technology be used to improve decision making?
3. In what situations would the use of technology not be appropriate, even potentially harmful, if used to facilitate decision making?

Instructor's Notes

B. **The Delphi Technique: Decisions by Expert Consensus**
   1. It is a technique developed by the Rand Corporation for collecting and organizing the opinions of several experts into a single decision.
   2. The steps of the process are presented in Figure 10-13. The Delphi Group: A Summary.
   3. It has the advantage of collecting expert judgments at relatively low cost. Its disadvantage is it is very time consuming. It also lacks a confirmation of the acceptance of the decision.

C. **The Nominal Group Technique: A Structured Group Meeting**
   1. This technique brings a small group, 7-10, together who systematically share their solutions and reactions to solutions.
   2. The process is outlined in Figure 10-14. The Nominal Group Technique: An Overview.
   3. It has the advantages of being fast and non-threatening. It has the disadvantages of needing trained leaders and only being suitable to handle one problem at a time.
   4. The technique is being used with electronic meetings, as well, with some success. See Figure 10-15. An Electronic Meeting in Progress at the Marriot Corporation.
   5. It lacks a confirmation of acceptance of the decision.

D. **The Stepladder Technique: Systematically Incorporating New Members**
   1. Is a technique to aid presentation of ideas to new group members.
   2. The process is summarized in Figure 10-16. The Stepladder Technique: A Summary.
   3. When using the technique, adequate time must be allowed for each person to work on the problem before meeting as a group.
   4. The process forces everyone to present ideas without knowing what the group has decided.
   5. Often members of these groups feel more positive about their experience.

> **You Be the Consultant**
> 1. Students can suggest any one of the various techniques, Delphi, nominal, the electronic variation, or the stepladder. Key is students' understanding the tradeoffs, the benefits versus the drawbacks of each and why they would make the choice they make.
> 2. Consider elaborating the situation with what the desired group outcome is, how much time is available, etc., to give the students opportunity to narrow their choices, given the different contexts.

Summary and Review

Questions For Discussion

1. Argue pro or con: "All people make decisions in the same manner."
   Answer - The correct answer is con, but you may have some students who don't buy into decision styles. The arguments will vary by students, but should tie in both decision style and the different types of decisions people face.

2. Think of any decision you recently made. Would you characterize it as programmed or nonprogrammed? Highly certain or highly uncertain? Top-down or empowered? Explain your answers.
   Answer - Answers will vary by student. Students need to understand the criteria for the different categories. Carefully question and listen to justifications for the classification of their decisions. Also note, what is one type of question for one student in one context may be a different type in another context for another student.

3. Describe a decision that you are likely to make following the administrative model and one that you are likely to make using the intuitive approach of image theory.
   Answer - Answers will vary. Help students think through the satisficing and bounded rationality aspects of their example for the administrative model. Are both present? With their image theory example, ask them to talk about how they made their compatibility and profitability tests. Ask for the context--decision frame--of the decision as well.

4. Identify ways in which decisions you have made may have been biased by framing, heuristics, the use of implicit favorites, and the escalation of commitment.
   Answer - Answers will vary widely. Look for the students' understanding of the concepts. Tie this question to #5. It should show that there are various answers depending on the elements mentioned here.

5. Imagine that you are a manager facing the problem of not attracting enough high-quality personnel to your organization. Would you attempt to solve this problem alone or by committee? Explain your reasoning.
   Answer - Students' answers should vary based on how they frame the question etc. If you aren't attracting candidates because you are writing poor ads, that's an individual problem. If people are not applying because the company has a bad reputation as a place of work, that's a group problem.

6. Groupthink is a potentially serious impediment to group decision making. Describe this phenomenon, and review some things that can be done to avoid it.

   Answer - Groupthink comes when members are highly cohesive, there is pressure to agree, a reluctance to question, an illusion of agreement, and a failure to consider alternatives. See Figure 10-12. Groupthink: An Overview. Students should suggest some of the following strategies for avoiding groupthink. 1) Promote open inquires. 2) Use subgroups. 3) Admit shortcomings. 4) Hold second-chance meetings.

7. Suppose you find out that a certain important organizational decision has to be made by a group, but you suspect that a better decision might be made by an individual. Describe three different ways you could use groups to make a decision while avoiding many of the problems associated with groups.

   Answer - The techniques would be Delphi, nominal group, and stepladder. Make students describe them, including benefits and disadvantages. Solutions will vary by students.

Case in Point: Communicating All the Right Messages at General Motors

1. Using the analytical model of decision making, how do you think the process unfolded to decide to change Coca-Cola's formula?

   Answer - Students may apply the model in various ways. The fundamental error was probably in problem identification which led to a poor solution, reformulate Coke.

2. What did Coca-Cola Co. do to reduce the uncertainty that surrounded its decision to change the formula?

   Answer - Note the heavy use of market research, polls, expert advice, and they took their time.

3. Do you agree with the one bottler's observation that executives more familiar with American culture may have made a different decision? Explain your answer.

   Answer - Students can argue pro and con. Listen for ethnocentrism in the discussion. The Japanese have better understood American consumers for years.

4. Do you think groupthink may have been involved in the decision? Explain how it may have operated in this context.

   Answer - On the one hand, it is hard to argue for groupthink with the diverse group of executives involved in the decision. On the other, it is hard to imagine how much pressure those executives were probably feeling to conform to a 'pre-made' decision.

Skills Portfolios

Experiencing Organizational Behavior

What Is Your Personal Decision Style?

1. Conduct as directed. Consider photocopying or retyping the questions to eliminate the possibility of the students reading the scoring instructions.
2. Remind students that a seven-question instrument is hardly definitive in describing their behavior but a fun way to start thinking about it.
3. Again, as with previous style instruments, consider having students record what they think their style is. After they take the instrument, consider having them poll three friends by describing the styles and asking their friends what style they are. These are ways to help the students accept the feedback they get from the instrument, particularly if they have a bias for or against a particular style.

Questions for Discussion
1. Discuss as directed.

<u>Working in Groups</u>
Running a Nominal Group: Try It Yourself
1. Use a topic offered in the text. The focus here is the technique, not the problem/topic.
2. Letting students offer other topics has a plus--they'll be more involved in the discussion--and a downside--they could suggest an inappropriate or highly volatile topic where the technique gets lost in the content.
3. Reduce the group size to 5 unless your facilitators are skilled at drawing people in. A group of 10 permits students to avoid discussion.
4. Outline the steps from Figure 9-5 on the board or give handouts to the facilitators.
5. Hold discussion to 25-30 minutes so you can discuss the questions below in the same class period. Students will forget what happened in the group from one class period to another two days later.
6. Appoint a recorder who notes behavior and the groups' answer.

Questions for Discussion
1. Have the recorders of each group briefly, in 2-3 minutes, describe the group's answer/decision before discussing Questions # 1 and 2.
2. Before Question #3, have the recorder or members of the group report problems they observed. Record the problems on the board, noting after each how many groups experienced similar problems.
3. Discuss Questions #4 and 5 as directed.

CHAPTER 11 - Helping, Cooperation, and Conflict in Organizations

Learning Objectives
After reading this chapter, you should be able to

1. Distinguish between *prosocial behavior* and *altruism*.
2. Describe *organizational citizenship behavior* and the major forms it often takes.
3. Explain the nature of *whistle-blowing* and describe some of the ethical issues it raises.
4. Describe the basic nature of *cooperation* and describe both individual and organizational factors that influence its occurrence.
5. Define *trust* and explain its relationship to both organization citizenship behavior and cooperation.
6. Define *conflict* and indicate how it can produce positive as well as negative effects.
7. Describe various styles of managing conflict and the basic dimensions that underlie them.
8. List several organizational and interpersonal causes of conflict.
9. Describe several effective means for managing conflict.
10. Distinguish between *workplace violence* and *workplace aggression*.
11. Describe causes of workplace aggression and techniques for reducing this harmful form of organizational behavior.

Chapter Contents   Page

Introduction
I.   Prosocial Behavior: Helping Others at Work   369
     A. Organizational Citizenship Behavior: Some Basic Forms   370
     B. Organizational Citizenship Behavior: Factors Affecting Its Occurrence 370
     C. Effects of OCB: Does It Really Matter?   372
     D. Whistle-Blowing: Helping an Organization by Dissenting with It   372

II. Cooperation: Mutual Assistance in Work Settings   374
     A. Individual Factors and Cooperation   374
     B. Organizational Factors and Cooperation   378
     C. Cooperation across Organizations   379

III. Conflict: Its Nature, Causes, and Effects   380
     A. Integration and Distribution: Two Basic Dimensions of Conflict   381
     B. The Major Causes of Conflict   381
     C. The Effects of Conflict: Definitely a Mixed Bag   384

IV. Conflict Management: Increasing the Benefits and Minimizing the Costs   386
     A. Bargaining: The Universal Process   386
     B. Third-Party Intervention: Mediation and Arbitration   388
     C. The Induction of Superordinate Goals   389

V.   Workplace Violence and Workplace Aggression   389
   A. Workplace Violence: The Tip of the Iceberg?   391
   B. The Causes of Workplace Aggression   392
   C. The Prevention and Control of Workplace Aggression   393

Summary and Review   394
Questions for Discussion   395
Case in Point   395
Skills Portfolio   396
   Experiencing Organizational Behavior   396
   Working in Groups   396

Chapter Outline

Instructor's Notes

Case Preview: Rubbermaid focused on its needs rather than taking a cooperative approach and looking at its needs and its customers' needs. Instead of working together to face a changing market Rubbermaid took an adversarial stance with its customers. Lesson learned, cooperation is more profitable than confrontation.

Introduction
1. Cooperation is a process by which individuals or organizations seek to coordinate their efforts in order to maximize joint outcomes or reach shared goals.
2. Companies often have a choice between confrontation and cooperation.
3. The chapter covers:
    *   what factors lead a company to choose cooperation or confrontation.
    *   the three basic processes of interaction; prosocial, cooperation, and conflict.
    *   workplace aggression and violence.
    *   strategies for reducing and dealing with workplace aggression and violence.

I.   Prosocial Behavior: Helping Others at Work
   A. Organizational Citizenship Behavior: Some Basic Forms
     1. OCB are actions by organizational members that exceed the formal requirements of their job and are, therefore, "above and beyond the call of duty."
     2. OCB has three major components.
       *   They exceed role requirements.
       *   They are discretionary in nature.
       *   They are not generally recognized by the formal reward structure.
     3. Not all experts agree on all three components.

4. Some believe that certain forms of prosocial behavior, categorized as **Organizational spontacity,** are OCB actions that are recognized by the formal reward structure.

5. There are five categories of OCB:
   - altruism.
   - conscientiousness.
   - civic virtue.
   - sportsmanship.
   - courtesy.
   - See Table 11-1. Specific Forms of Organizational Citizenship Behavior.

B. **Organizational Citizenship Behavior: Factors Affecting Its Occurrence**
   1. What factors play a role in OCB?
      - Trust by employees that they will be treated fairly.
      - The degree to which supervisors' decisions follow the principles of distributive and procedural fairness.
      - Strongly related to employees' perceptions of the breadth of their jobs, what their roles are.
      - Their perceptions of any punishment received, if it is fair or not.

You Be the Consultant
1. There are a variety of ways the HR Director could find out by legitimate means--employee surveys, confrontation meetings, to illegitimate means tap into the grapevine through informants, etc. Help the students focus on appropriate means.
2. This would call for a significant company-wide effort. Everything from the compensation and rewards systems to discipline processes would need to be reviewed for their fairness and equity. Students should see that fixing this problem is no small task.

C. **Effects of OCB: Does It Really Matter?**
   1. There are three ingredients in organizational effectiveness.
      - Recruiting and retaining excellent employees.
      - Employees accomplishing their jobs.
      - Employees engaging in innovative, spontaneous activity beyond the scope of their immediate jobs.
   2. All the points are effected by OCB and the third ingredient relates to it directly.
   3. The difficulty is that most of the elements of OCB are not standards of measurement, not part of the formal reward system. By definition, it is hard to track OCB's contribution to organizations.

D. **Whistle-Blowing: Helping an Organization by Dissenting with It**
   1. Whistle-Blowing is the disclosure by employees of illegal, immoral, or illegitimate practice by employers.

2. The consequence is often punishment for the whistle-blower.
    *   Harassment.
    *   Transfer to a less desirable job.
    *   Firing.
    *   Retaliation.
3. Is Whistle-blowing prosocial behavior? Many would say yes because most of the time whistle-blowers are seeking the redress of a wrong rather than grinding a personal ax.

The Ethics Angle
The Costs of Whistle Blowing
1. This case provides an excellent opportunity to discuss the reasons for whistle-blowing and the reality of the consequences.
2. Students may be a bit utilitarian, why do it if it's such a hassle? Help them see that it's the right thing to do and that the individual, the company, and the consumer eventually benefit. The individual retains his/her personal integrity. The company does the right thing and stops expending the resources to hide its improper behavior. And, the consumer receives better products and service and can trust the company.

II. Cooperation: Mutual Assistance in Group Settings
    The age-old dilemma in business, "do we cooperate or compete," has traditionally been answered, compete. There are times when competition is the right answer. But there are times when cooperation works more effectively.

A. **Individual Factors and Cooperation**
    1. There are a number of factors facilitating cooperation the most important are reciprocity and personal characteristics.
    2. Reciprocity is simply responding to others' behavior in kind. It is the guiding principle of cooperation.
    3. Trust is a powerful antecedent to cooperation. When an individual has confidence and a belief that the good will of management will help in the accomplishment of mutually beneficial goals, you have **trust.**
    4. There are two types of trust.
        *   Cognition-based trust which refers to our beliefs about others' reliability and trustworthiness.
        *   Affect-based trust refers to the emotional bond between individuals.
        *   See Figure 11-3. Trust Cooperation, and Job Performance.
    6. People fall into four groups in terms of their orientations toward cooperation or competition.
        *   Competitors - prime motive to be better than others.
        *   Individualists - little interest in others' outcomes.
        *   Cooperators - want to maximize joint success.
        *   Equalizers - their goal is to minimize differences.
        *   See Figure 11.4. Personal Orientations Toward Working with Others.

Globalization and Diversity in Today's Organizations
Trust: Does It Differ Around the World?
1. An excellent opportunity to show how the definition of a word changes perspectives and application.
2. Students should note the significant differences in assumptions about people and behavior between the two cultures.

Instructor's Notes

7. Another dimension along which people differ is **individualism-collectivism.**
    *   See Figure 11.5. Collectivism, Individualism, and Cooperation.

B. **Organizational Factors and Cooperation**
    1. Reward systems and organizational structure also contribute to cooperation or competition. If a reward system is "winner-take-all," then competition will be fostered.
    2. Interdependence among employees is a function of the nature of their different jobs. If their job structure fosters competition or requires cooperation, that's what the organization will get.

C. **Cooperation across Organizations**
    1. There are times when organizations agree to cooperate with each other.
        *   When independent companies conclude they could greatly increase their gains by cooperation.
        *   When one or more competitors enters a mature and stable market.
        *   When the environment is rapidly changing.

III. Conflict: Its Nature, Causes, and Effects
    1. **Conflict** is a process by which one party perceives that another party has taken some action that will exert negative effects on its major interest, or is about to take such actions.
    2. Key elements to conflict:
        *   opposing interests.
        *   recognition of such opposition.
        *   belief that each side will try to thwart the other.
        *   actions occur that do thwart the other party.
    3. Practicing managers spend 20% of their time dealing with conflict.
    A. **Integration and Distribution: Two Basic Dimensions of Conflict**
        1. Distribution - concern with one's own outcomes.
        2. Integration - concern with the outcomes of others.

3. Five styles of handling conflict.
   - <u>Compromise</u> - Split issues down the middle.
   - <u>Competition</u> - high concern with one's own interests.
   - <u>Collaboration</u> - high concern for one's own interest and those of others.
   - <u>Accommodation</u> - giving others what they want.
   - <u>Avoidance</u> - low concern for oneself and others.
   - See Figure 11-7. Basic Styles of Resolving Conflict.
4. Organizational causes of conflict:
   - Competition over scarce resources.
   - Ambiguity over responsibility.
   - Ambiguity over jurisdiction.
   - Interdependence between work units.
   - Competitive reward systems.
   - Differentiation.
   - Power differentials.
   - See Figure 11-8. Organizational Causes of Conflict.
5. Interpersonal causes of organizational conflict.
   - Grudges - seeking revenge for past hurts.
   - Faulty attributions about others' motivation.
   - Faulty communication. See Table 11-2. Constructive versus Destructive Criticism.
   - Distrust.
   - Personal Characteristics.

B. **Major Causes of Conflict**
   1. Organizational causes of conflict.
      - Competing over scarce resources.
      - Ambiguity over responsibility.
      - Ambiguity over jurisdiction.
   2. Interpersonal causes of organizational conflict.
      - Grudges.
      - Faulty attributions.
      - Faulty communication.
         - Inappropriate criticism. Distructive versus constructive.
      - Distrust.
      - Personal characteristics.
         - Type A versus Type B.
         - Self-monitoring.

C. **The Effects of Conflict: Definitely a Mixed Bag**
   1. The negative effects of conflict.
      - Interferes with communication.
      - Creates strong negative emotions.
      - Diverts attention from productive efforts.

- May cause participative leader to become authoritarian.
- Encourages negative stereotyping.
- Fosters groupthink and narrow-minded loyalty.

2. The positive effects of conflict.
   - Brings hidden problems into the open.
   - Motivates mutual understanding.
   - Encourages consideration of new ideas and approaches.
   - Can lead to better decisions.
   - Enhances group loyalty (but see "g" above).
   - Can enhance organizational commitment.

IV. <u>Conflict Management: Increasing the Benefits and Minimizing the Costs</u>
   A. **Bargaining: The Universal Process**
      1. This is the process of exchanging offers, counteroffers, and concessions. If successful, all sides attain an acceptable solution.
      2. Specific tactics. These are designed to reduce opponents' aspirations in order to induce acceptance of an offer favorable to your side.
      3. Framing is the cognitive set, or focus, adopted by bargainers. It is how they perceive or define the situation. There are three key dimensions.
         - Relationship/task.
         - Emotional/intellectual.
         - Cooperative/win.
         - See Figure 11-11. Cognitive Frames in Bargaining.
      3. A third important aspect of negotiations is the perceptions of the situation. There are several important common misperceptions in bargaining.
         - The <u>incompatibility</u> error - the view that the two sides' interests are incompatible.
         - The <u>fixed-sum</u> error - the view that each side places the same emphasis or importance on every element of the negotiation.
      4. Perhaps the single most important factor in successful negotiating is the participants' orientation, win-win versus win-lose.
         - <u>Win-lose</u> - one side gains only at the expense of the other.
         - <u>Win-win</u> - both sides can have what they really want. Not all situations lend themselves to win-win, but it is often an achievable goal.
         - See Table 11-3. Techniques for Reaching Integrative Agreements.

B. **Third-Party Intervention: Mediation and Arbitration**
 1. Mediation is third party intervention where the neutral third-party tries to facilitate agreement.
    - Seeks voluntary agreements.
    - No formal power, seeks to clarify.
    - Cannot impose agreement, may offer specific recommendations.
    - Role is facilitator.
 2. Arbitration is an interventions where the third party has the power to impose a resolution. There are several types.
    - <u>Binding</u> - parties agree in advance to accept terms.
    - <u>Voluntary</u> - parties may reject terms.
    - <u>Conventional</u> - arbitrator offers terms.
    - <u>Final-offer</u> - arbitrator chooses from terms offered by disputants.
 3. Drawbacks of mediation and arbitration.
    - Mediation often proves ineffective because it requires cooperation.
    - Arbitration may inhibit serious bargaining; parties may suspect that the arbitrator is biased, it is expensive; and the commitment to a settlement may be lower than to a negotiated one.

C. **The Induction of Superordinate Goals**
 1. One way to counter the common experience of being in "different camps," is the pursuit of **superordinate goals.** These are goals that tie the two sides together.
 2. If the two conflicting parties have to focus on, and work toward, common objectives, barriers will be weakened.

The Quest for Quality
<u>When Suppliers Become Partners--Not Adversaries</u>
1. Solid examples of the positive results of cooperation. What are the legal implications, any anti-trust issues?
2. Review the three steps offered, then discuss with students what other steps companies can take to cooperatively reach their goals.

V. <u>Workplace Violence and Workplace Aggression</u>
 Workplace violence--direct physical assaults by present or former employees against other people in their organizations--has been increasing.
A. **Workplace Violence: The Tip of the Iceberg?**
 1. Most workplace violence involves outsiders entering a business for criminal purposes and harming the employees.
 2. There is a growing problem of **workplace aggression**, efforts by individuals to harm others with whom they work.
    - Verbal and physical, passive or active, and indirect or direct.

<u>Instructor's Notes</u>

B. The Causes of Workplace Aggression

1. There are many causes that often fit into four large categories.
   - The characteristics of the individuals who perpetrate the aggression.
   - Interpersonal issues, perception of unfair treatment, not getting along, etc.
   - Unpleasant environmental working conditions.
   - The result of a significant change in the organization.

C. The Prevention and Control of Workplace Aggression

1. There are a number of things that can be done to cut down on workplace violence and aggression.
   - Careful screening of prospective employees.
   - Establishing clear disciplinary procedures for such behavior.
   - Assuring high levels of organizational justice.
   - Training employees how to respond to threats of violence.

Summary and Review

Questions For Discussion

1. <u>What kind of organizational citizenship behaviors have you observed in your own work experience? Why, if individuals receive no direct benefit for engaging in such actions, do they ever perform them?</u>
   Answer - Answers will vary by student. Students should apply specific reasons to each incident they share, not just list the reason. Such behavior is not reinforced by the formal rewards system.

2. <u>What factors in an organization might lead to high levels of trust between employees? Would it be worthwhile to assure that these factors are present?</u>
   Answer - The factors that play a role in OCB are: a) trust by employees that they will be treated fairly, b) the degree to which supervisors' decisions follow the principles of distributive and procedural fairness, c) employees' perceptions of the breadth of their jobs, what their roles are, d) employee perceptions of the fairness of any punishment received. It is worthwhile, but students should note that it's sometimes hard to prove quantitatively.

3. <u>What are the ethical issues one must consider when deciding whether or not to blow the whistle on an organization suspected of some wrongdoing?</u>
   Answer - The potential consequences to the whistle-blower: 1) Harassment, 2) transfer to less desirable job, 3) firing, 4) retaliation. Help the students realize that while it is only rational to think through the consequences, they still need to do the right thing. Evil wins because good men and women do nothing.

4. What role do cultural factors play in cooperation? In other words, would you expect to observe different levels of cooperation in different cultures? Why?

    Answer - Students should draw from the Globalization case on the differences between the U.S. and Japan. Ask students for other cultural experiences they've had. Prepare an example from a European and an Asian culture to facilitate discussion.

5. Do you think that individuals differ with respect to their preferred modes of resolving conflicts (e.g., compromise, collaboration, competition)? Would these differences show up in all situations, or only under certain circumstances?

    Answer - As this is discussed, have students discuss particular disagreements they've had or observed, and what different behaviors and perspectives they saw. How people respond does follow a pattern but is influenced by circumstances, so differences do occur in all situations and sometimes only under certain circumstances.

6. "Conflict doesn't exist until it is recognized by the parties involved." Do you agree with this statement? Why or why not?

    Answer - Students answers will vary. Basically, conflict exists if one party has a problem with another, if there are opposing interests, etc. The text definition suggests both sides need to recognize opposition and believe that each side will try to thwart the other, but in reality, if someone thinks there is a conflict, there is.

7. Growing evidence indicates that conflict can sometimes produce positive results. Have you ever experienced positive results? If so, why do you think such an effect occurred?

    Answer - Students may need help seeing the positive outcomes of conflict. 1) Brings hidden problems into the open. 2) Motivates mutual understanding. 3) Encourages consideration of new ideas and approaches. 4) Can lead to better decisions. 5) Enhances group loyalty 6) Can enhance organizational commitment.

8. If people in your organization are frequently in conflict with each other, what techniques could you use to reduce the number or intensity of these conflicts?

    Answer - Answers will vary from dealing with the sources of organizational and interpersonal conflict to developing superordinate goals.

9. Do you think that workplace violence and workplace aggression are increasing? If so, why? If not, why?

    Answer - The answer depends on whether students focus on workplace violence, which is increasing, or workplace aggression, which is fairly stable. Also, how it is defined is important. Note that the text groups everything from physical abuse to not writing down phone messages as workplace aggression. Help the students be clear on what they mean by it.

Case in Point: When Rivals Become Mortal Enemies: How Sony Used the "Ultimate Weapon" in Thailand.

1. Do you think the price-cutting tactics used by Sony are ethical? If so, why? If not, why?

    Answer - Students will argue both sides. Be sure students do not fall back on the rationale that since it's not illegal, it's not unethical.

2. How could Matsushita have fought back when it discovered what Sony was doing? Or was it already too late once Sony had launched its strategy?

     Answer - Matsushi could cut prices, offer better service, niche market, withdraw from the market, attack Sony in a different market to distract them, negotiate a cooperative relationship.

3. What counterattack do you think Matsushita should adopt now, given that it has lost an important market segment to Sony?

     Answer - Answers will vary.

Skills Portfolios
Experiencing Organizational Behavior
Personal Styles of Conflict Management
1. Administer as directed.

Questions for Discussion
1. Discuss as directed.

Working in Groups
The Good Mood-Helping Effect: One Reason Why "Wineing and Dining" Others Often Works
1. Photocopy the roles, cut in half, and only give the half to the person playing the role.
2. Photocopy the evaluation form and give copies to the persons playing the interviewer role.

Questions for Discussion
1. Discuss as directed.

Chapter 12 - Influence, Power, and Politics in Organizations

Learning Objectives
After reading this chapter, you should be able to
1. Distinguish among *social influence*, *power*, and *politics* in organizations.
2. Characterize the major varieties of social influence that exist.
3. Describe the conditions under which social influence is used.
4. Identify the major types of individual power in organizations and the conditions under which power is used.
5. Explain the two major approaches to the development of subunit power in organizations (the *resource-dependency* model and the *strategic contingencies* model).
6. Describe when and where *organizational politics* is likely to occur and the forms it is likely to take.
7. Explain the major ethical issues surrounding the uses of power and political behavior in organizations.

Chapter Contents

	Page
Introduction	
I. Organizational Influence, Power, and Politics: Some Key Distinctions	402
II. Social Influence: Having an Impact on Others	403
A. Tactics of Social Influence	403
B. Putting Influence Tactics to Work	404
III. Individual Power: A Basis for Influence	405
A. Position Power: Influence That Comes with the Office	405
B. Personal Power: Influence That Comes from the Individual	407
C. Power: How Is It Used?	409
D. Empowerment: The Shifting Bases of Power in Today's Organizations	411
IV. Group or Subunit Power: Structural Determinants	413
A. The Resource-Dependency Model: Controlling Critical Resources	413
B. The Strategic Contingencies Model: Power Through Dependence	414
V. Organizational Politics: Power in Action	417
A. Political Tactics: What Forms Do They Take?	417
B. When Does Political Action Occur?	420
C. Organizational Politics: Where in the Organization Does it Occur?	422
D. Political Behavior: Is It Ethical?	422
Summary and Review	427
Questions for Discussion	428
Case in Point	428
Skills Portfolio	429
Experiencing Organizational Behavior	429
Working in Groups	430

Chapter Outline

Instructor's Notes

Case Preview: The case presents an interesting contrast, the benefits of having a super power in computing like Microsoft with the negatives of having the ability to ruin entire companies. Can a company or a business person become too large and powerful?

Introduction
1. The effort to get others to behave in a certain way is known as **social influence.** This largely depends on the use of power.
2. The Bill Gates, Microsoft story is a classic example of organizational politics, the use of power and influence.
3. The chapter:
   - begins by distinguishing among influence, power, and politics.
   - discusses the tactics used to influence others within an organization.
   - examines how power is attained and used.
   - considers ethical issues in the use of organizational power.

I. Organizational Influence, Power, and Politics: Some Key Distinctions
1. Social influence is the attempt to influence others.
   - See Figure 12-1. Relationship among Social Influence, Power, and Politics.
2. Power is the potential to influence others. It is the capacity to change the behavior or attitudes of another in a desired fashion.
3. Organizational politics is the unauthorized use of power to protect or enhance one's own interests.

II. Social Influence: Having an Impact on Others
   A. **Tactics of Social Influence**
   1. There are a number of techniques for social influence.
      - Rational persuasion.
      - Inspirational appeal.
      - Consultation.
      - Ingratiation.
      - Exchange - promising benefits for compliance.
      - Personal Appeal.
      - Coalition building.
      - Legitimizing - using one's authority.
      - Pressure - use of threats or demands.
   2. Any of the techniques work. The most popular ones are:
      - rational persuasion.
      - inspirational appeal.
      - consultation.
   3. The least desireable are:
      - Legitimizing and Pressure.

B. **Putting Influence Tactics to Work**
1. People tend to use appeal and ingratiation when influencing upward if the boss is authoritarian, but use rational appeal if the boss is participative.

III. Individual Power: A Basis for Influence
A. **Position Power: Influence That Comes with the Office**
1. Position power is the formal power one has because of his/her position/job. Position power has four bases.
   - Legitimate power - people recognize and accept your authority.
   - Reward power - you control the rewards people value.
   - Coercive power - comes from the ability to control the punishments people can receive.
   - Information power - is based on the data and other knowledge the individual holds.

B. **Personal Power: Influence That Comes from the Individual**
1. Personal power flows from the unique characteristics or qualities of the individual.
   - Rational persuasion uses factual evidence and logical arguments to influence.
   - Expert power is based on superior knowledge.
   - Referent power is based on liking and respect for the individual.
   - Charisma is based on the individual's personality, the ability to be engaging and magnetic.
   - See Figure 12-3. Types of Individual Power: A Summary.

Globalization and Diversity in Today's Organizations
How Strong is Peer Influence? Comparing the United States and Denmark
1. Discuss the concept of **false-consensus effect,** ask students for examples of this phenomenon on campus to test their understanding of it.
2. Students should note that cultural attitudes and values influence each other. The competitive and individualistic orientation of the U.S. results in a greater concern about social comparison.
3. This should suggest to students that influence tactics need to be adjusted for the culture as well as for the individual.

C. **Power: How is it Used?**
1. The various bases of power are not entirely separate. A manager who uses expert power will enhance his/her legitimate power at the same time.
2. How people choose to use power is a complex question. Figure 12-5. American CEOs: What Are Their Power Bases, gives a snapshot of how one group chooses its power bases.
3. Expert power is preferred among peers and superiors.

4. Coercive power is frowned on in general.

D. **Empowerment: The Shifting Basis of Power in Today's Organizations**
   1. Power is shifting from managers to employees, from centralized leadership to decentralized.
   2. The passing of responsibility and authority to employees is the concept of **empowerment**. The manager-employee relationship shifts.
      - Bosses become facilitators and teachers.
      - They ask questions versus telling employees what to do.
   3. While talked about a great deal, empowerment is not yet widely practiced.

IV. Groups or Subunit Power: Structural Determinants
   A. **The Resource-Dependency Model: Controlling Critical Resources**
      1. This model views the organization as a set of subunits.
      2. The subunits are in relationship with one another, and some control resources other subunits need.
      3. Subunits controlling more resources than others are seen as more powerful. Such an imbalance, or *asymmetry,* is normal.
      4. Power is based on the degree to which the subunit controls the resources required by other units.
      5. The key determinant is control of needed resources. See Figure 12-7. The Resource-Dependency Model: An Example.

   B. **The Strategic Contingencies Model: Power Through Dependence**
      1. This model looks at interdependency among subunits based on which department's actions affect other departments, and whose actions are contingent upon another's actions.
      2. These contingencies are controlled by different departments depending on the industry.
      3. There are three primary factors that give subunits control over strategic contingencies.
         - If subunits have the capacity to reduce uncertainty.
         - If subunits have a high degree of centrality in the organization.
         - If the subunits' activities are nonsubstitutable and indispensable.
         - See Figure 12-9. Strategic Contingencies Model: Identifying Sources of Subunit Power.

V. Organizational Politics: Power in Action

Organizational politics tend to involve placing one's self-interests above the intersts of the organization.

A. **Political Tactics: What Forms Do They Take?**
   1. Six techniques are most often used in organizational politics.
      - Controlling access to information.
      - Cultivating a favorable impression.
      - Developing a base of support.
      - Blaming and attacking others.
      - Aligning oneself with more powerful others.
      - Playing political games.
   2. Political games in organizations take a number of forms.
      - Authority games.
        - Insurgency (resisting authority).
        - Counterinsurgency.
      - Power-based games.
        - Sponsorship.
        - Alliance.
        - Empire building.
      - Rivalry games.
        - Line vs. staff.
        - Rival camps.
      - Change games.
        - Whistle-blowing.
        - Young Turks.
      - See Table 12-1. Political Games: A Summary of Some Examples.

B. **When Does Political Action Occur?**
   1. When does political action take place?
      - There is a high level of uncertainty.
      - Large amounts of scarce resources are at stake.
      - There are conflicting interests.
      - Parties involved have equal power.
   2. Politics in human resource management occurs in:
      - performance appraisals.
      - personnel selection.
      - compensation decisions.
   6. An organization's life span affects the level and type of organizational politics played.
      - At birth and in early growth, power is gained through the putting forward of ideas in a rational manner.
      - At maturity, political means increase as various departments compete for resources.
      - In decline or redevelopment, political activity is at its greatest as people and units fight for survival.

<u>Instructor's Notes</u>

C. **Organizational Politics: Where in the Organization Does It Occur?**
1. Wherever there is a lack of clear policies.
2. Wherever there is a high level of ambiguity.
3. See Figure 12-10.

You Be the Consultant
1. There are number of ways they could interfere. People could hinder each other's performance, not cooperate when necessary, hide or miscommunicate essential information, not communicate as often or thoroughly as needed, etc.
2. Students could argue for a variety of location but most clearly in areas where, there is a high level of uncertainty, large amounts of scarce resources are at stake, there are conflicting interests, and when the parties involved have equal power.
3. Students can argue for a variety of political games. See Table 12-1.

<u>Instructor's Notes</u>

D. **Political Behavior: Is It Ethical?**
1. There are a number of consideration when assessing the ethics of organizational politics. See Figure 12-11. Guidelines for Determining Ethical Action.
2. Political behavior is ethical if it meets three criteria:
    - Does it foster organizational interests over individual greed?
    - Does it respect the rights of the individual?
    - Does the action conform to the standards of equity and justice, is it fair?
        - Sometimes more powerful people will work to convince others (and themselves) that what they are doing is ethical.
5. Survey HR professionals were most concerned about:
    - abuse of power, especially in personnel decisions or basing pay on friendships.
    - making arrangements with vendors for personal gain.
    - See Figure 12-12. Political Antics Top the "Most Unethical List": Survey Results.
5. The self-serving nature of these actions make they especially difficult for managers to address.
    - Only 10% of managers attribute unethical behavior to political pressure.
    - 56% attribute unethical behavior to the attitudes and behaviors of senior managmenet.
6. There may be occasions when violating standards of justice are valid.
    - Giving a higher than justified pay raise to motivate.

The Quest For Quality

Coping With Organizational Politics: Some Techniques

1. An excellent practical series of steps to take to combat politics.
2. Discuss with students their reactions to these thoughts and how real they feel they are.
3. Can students offer other suggestions? What experiences have they had in dealing with organizational politics on their jogs, in their social groups, dealing with the administration of your institution.

Summary and Review

Questions For Discussion

1. Suppose your profession asks you to redo a homework assignment. Explain the various bases of individual social power he/she may use to influence your behavior in this situation.

   Answer - There are any number of techniques for social influence he/she could use: rational persuasion, exchange - promising benefits for compliance, personal appeal, legitimizing - using one's authority, or pressure - use of threats or demands.

2. Using the resource-dependency model and the strategic contingencies model as the basis for your analysis, describe the relative power differences between groups in any organization with which you are familiar.

   Answer - Students' answers will vary for the resource-dependency model they need to show that some controls, the resources required by other units, and that the key determinant is control of needed resources. See Figure 12-7. The Resource-Dependency Model: An Example. For the strategic contingencies model, the key to demonstrate is the interdependency among subunits based on which department's actions affect other departments, and whose actions are contingent upon another's actions. Also, that these contingencies are controlled by different departments depending on the industry and that they mention the three primary factors that give subunits control over strategic contingencies. 1) If subunits have the capacity to reduce uncertainty. 2) If subunits have a high degree of centrality in the organization   : If the subunits' activities are nonsubstitutable and indispensable. See Figure 12-9. Strategic Contingencies Model: Identifying Sources of Subunit Power.

3. Describe the political tactics and tricks that one person may use to gain a power advantage over another in an organization.

   Answer - The students have six techniques to choose from. 1) Controlling access to information. 2) Cultivating a favorable impression. 3) Developing a base of support. 4) Blaming and attacking others. 5) Aligning oneself with more powerful others. 6) Playing political games.

4. Suppose you're the manager of a human resources department. Are political activities more likely or less likely to take place in your department compared to other departments? Why? What form might these actions be expected to take?

   Answer - Answers will vary by student.

5. Argue for or against this statement, "The use of power in organizations is unethical."

   Answer - Answers will vary by student.

6. Although it might not be possible to completely eliminate organizational politics, it might be possible to manage political activity effectively. Describe some of the things that can be done to cope with organizational politics.

    Answer - Students should tap into The Quest For Quality discussion of tactics, such as, clarify job expectations, be a good role model, do not turn a blind eye to game players, etc.

Case in Point:Chrysler's Battle for the Boardroom

1. What political tactics did Eaton use to defend himself against Kerkorian?

    Answer - Eaton built alliances, generated positive results, developed open communication, more participative, friendly leadership.

2. What bases of individual power does Eaton appear to have at his disposal?

    Answer - The use of information from position power, heavy use of personal power--expert and referent but not charismatic.

Skills Portfolios

Experiencing Organizational Behavior

What Kinds of Power Does Your Supervisor Use?

1. If students don't have a supervisor ask them to reference this against a previous supervisor they had or against a professor they had to work closely with.
2. Have students predict what types of power the supervisor/professor made greatest use of before they complete the questionnaire.
3. Score as directed.

Questions for Discussion

1. When discussing the questions ask students for the implications of a) their supervisor behaving in ways consistent with his/her main use of power and b) their supervisor acting in ways inconsistent with his/her main use of power.
2. Students may feel they've never supervised anyone, reference Question #3. Have them recall team class projects they lead, social organizations or social events they headed, etc. when discussing this question. Have them offer specific events, things they did that evidence the type of power they think they used.

Working in Groups

Recognizing Organizational Politics When You See It

1. Conduct as directed.

Questions for Discussion

1. Discuss as directed.

Chapter 13 - Leadership: Its Nature and Impact on Organizations

Learning Objectives

After reading this chapter you should be able to

1. Define *leadership*, and indicate why leading and managing are not always the same.
2. Describe traits that distinguish leaders from other people.
3. Describe various forms of participative and autocratic leader behavior.
4. Distinguish between the two basic forms of leader behavior: *person-oriented* behavior and *production-oriented* behavior.
5. Explain what the *leader-member* exchange (LMX) model says about the relationships between leaders and followers
6. Describe the role of *attribution* in the leadership process.
7. Describe the nature of *charismatic* leadership and how it compares to *transformational* leadership.
8. Appreciate the special considerations involved in leading teams.
9. Explain the general nature of *contingency theories* of leader effectiveness.
10. Summarize the basic nature of five different contingency theories: *LPC contingency theory, situational leadership theory, path-goal theory, normative decision theory*, and *substitutes for leadership theory.*

Chapter Contents

	Page
Introduction	
I. Leadership: Its Basic Nature	433
A. Leadership: A Working Definition	433
B. Leaders Versus Managers: A Key Distinction--At Least In Theory	434
II. Leader Traits and Behaviors	435
A. The Trait Approach: Having the "Right Stuff"	435
B. Permissive Versus Autocratic Leadership Behaviors	437
C. Person-Oriented Versus Production-Oriented Leaders	438
D. Developing Successful Leader Behaviors: Grid Training	440
III. Leaders and Followers	442
A. The Leader-Member Exchange (LMX) Model: The Importance of Being in the "In-Group"	442
B. The Attribution Approach: Leaders' Explanations of Followers' Behavior	443
C. Charismatic Leaders: That "Something Special"	444
D. Transformational Leadership: Beyond Charisma	447
E. Leading Teams: Special Considerations	448
IV. Contingency Theories of Leadership Effectiveness	450
A. LPC Contingency Theory: Matching Leaders and Tasks	451
B. Situational Leadership Theory: Adjusting Leadership Style to the Situation	453
C. Path-Goal Theory: Leaders as Guides to Valued Goals	455
D. Normative Decision Theory: The Right Time for Employee Participation	456
E. Substitutes for Leadership Theory: When Leaders Are Superfluous	459

Summary and Review   462
Questions for Discussion   463
Case in Point   464
Skills Portfolio   464
    Experiencing Organizational Behavior   464
    Working in Groups   465

Chapter Outline

Instructor's Notes

Case Preview: This sidebar case outlines the major steps of Jim Barksdale's leadership of Netscape into the market. Clearly, his aggressive leadership accounts for some of its success. But how much was a matter of being in the right place at the right time, rather than Barksdale's leadership? Could anyone else have done as much?

Introduction

1. Most executives feel that effective leadership is the number one factor in the success of an organization. Research seems to support this feeling.
2. Leadership is one of the most studied concepts in social science with over 10,000 books and articles published on the topic.
3. The chapter covers:
   - the differences between a manager and a leader.
   - the traits and behaviors that make leaders.
   - the major theories of leadership.
   - the conditions under which leaders are effective or ineffective.

I. Leadership: Its Basic Nature
   A. **Leadership: A Working Definition**
      1. Leadership is the process of influencing others in a group.
      2. It primarily deals with influencing behavior, attitudes, or actions of others.
      3. It also entails using influence for a purpose.
      4. It is a two-way street. As leaders influence subordinates, so subordinates influence leaders.

   B. **Leaders versus Managers: A Key Distinction - at Least in Theory**
      1. A leader creates mission and strategy.
      2. A manager implements that mission and strategy.
      3. These distinctions are sometimes blurred in practice. Some managers are leaders; there just isn't a clear linkage between the two roles.
      4. See Figure 13-2. Leaders and Managers: Distinguishing Their Roles.

II. Leadership Traits and Behaviors

A. **The Trait Approach: Having the "Right Stuff"**

1. Early researchers formulated the **great person theory**—that leaders possess key traits that make them different from other people. The key elements are:
   - key distinguishing traits.
   - the traits are stable over time.
   - it is true across time and groups.

2. The concept fit informal experience, but no research would verify the theory.

3. Recent research suggests that leaders do differ. See Table 13.1. Characteristics of Successful Leaders.

4. Kirkpatrick and Locke coined the term **leadership motivation,** the leader's desire to influence others, which comes in two forms.
   - Personalized power motivation, the desire to dominate others, demonstrated by an excessive concern with status.
   - Socialized power motivation focuses on achieving desired shared goals by cooperating with others and developing networks.

5. Other key traits are *cognitive ability* and *flexibility*. Leaders are high in both.

B. **Participative versus Autocratic Leadership Behaviors**

1. Most recognize that autocratic and permissive styles are two separate dimensions:
   - the extent to which leaders permit subordinates participate in decisions, this is the autocratic-democratic dimension.
   - the extent to which leaders direct the activities of subordinates, this is the permissive-directive dimension.

2. This results in four possible patterns of behavior.
   - Directive autocrat - makes decisions without consulting subordinates and supervises workers closely.
   - Permissive autocrat - makes decisions without consulting subordinates, but gives workers a high degree of freedom in their work.
   - Directive democrat - makes decisions with input from subordinates, but supervises workers closely.
   - Permissive democrat- makes decisions with input from subordinates and gives them a great deal of freedom in their work.
   - Each style works best in certain environments with certain types of work. The key is matching the style to the situation.
   - See Table 13-2. Contrasting Styles of Leadership.

C. **Person-Oriented versus Production-Oriented Leaders**

1. Research shows that leaders differ as to their concern with task or people.
2. Those focused on the first dimension, task, or **initiating structure**, are concerned with production, getting the job done, and engage in organizing work, inducing rule following, etc.
3. Those high in the second dimension, people, or **consideration**, are primarily concerned with good relations, being liked, and engage in doing favors, explaining, and assuring their welfare.
4. See Figure 13.3. Leader Behavior: Two Basic Dimensions.
5. Neither dimension is better than the other. Each fits particular circumstances, thereby establishing their effectiveness, except that people who are high in concern for production and people seem to do best.

D. **Developing Successful Leader Behaviors: Grid Training**

1. This is a multi-step process designed to cultivate these two traits.
2. The process begins by taking an instrument that determines where participants stand in relationship to their concern for production and their concern for people.
    *   Impoverished management is low in concern for production and low in concern for people.
    *   Task management is high in concern for production and low in concern for people.
    *   Country club management is low in concern for production and high in concern for people.
    *   Middle of the road management is moderate in concern for production and moderate in concern for people.
    *   See Figure 13-4. The Managerial Grid.

III. Leaders and Followers

A. **The Leader-Member Exchange (LMX) Model: The Importance of Being in the "In-Group"**

1. Leaders treat their subordinates differently. Graen and his associates developed the LMX Model to explain this behavior.
2. The **In-group:**
    *   are favored by leader.
    *   receive more attention and resources from leader.
    *   are expected to perform jobs better.
    *   hold a more positive attitude toward the job.
3. Those in the **Out-group** are disfavored, and therefore receive less time and resources from leader.

4. These groups are formed by the leader on minimal information. Members are added to the in-group for various reasons.
    *   Perceived similarity with respect to personal characteristics.
    *   Belief an individual is especially competent.

B. **The Attribution Approach: Leaders' Explanations of Followers' Behavior**
    1. How the leader sees his/her followers, the attribution made, affects followers behavior especially their job performance.
        *   The attribution process is most carefully carried out in cases of poor performance.
    2. The implication is that leadership lies as much in leaders' perceptions as the perceptions of those led.
    3. See Figure 13-6. Leaders' Attributions of Followers' Poor Performance.

C. **Charismatic Leaders: That "Something Special"**
    1. History has many examples of individuals who seem to possess unusual and special skills that equip them for leading others.
    2. Charismatic leaders are noted for several characteristics.
        *   Self-confidence.
        *   A vision.
        *   Extraordinary behavior.
        *   Recognized as Change Agents.
        *   Environmental sensitivity.
    3. Leaders are considered charismatic based on the performance of their followers.
        *   Above normal levels of performance.
        *   High levels of devotion, loyalty, reverence toward leader.
        *   Enthusiasm and excitement for the leader and leader's ideas.
    4. Because charismatic leaders are viewed as heroic, people are very satisfied with their leadership and do well under their leadership.
    5. Charismatic leadership does have its downside, historically, when the leader is misguided. Also, charismatic leadership does not always fit in organizations.
    6. People's reactions to charismatic leaders tends to be polarized. People love them or hate them.

The Ethics Angle

Northrop Keeps Tabs on Leaders' Ethics

1. Notice how the current organizational behavior, keeping tabs on ethics, is a response to past problems.
2. Northrop's situation shows that even leaders need checks and balances on their behavior.
3. Discuss with students the results of the surveys and the apparent improvement of leaders' scores. What could the increase in scores indicate, besides the fact the leaders are acting more ethically?

<u>Instructor's Notes</u>

D. **Transformational Leadership: Beyond Charisma**
   1. Transformational leaders have the charisma of the charismatic leader, but other qualities as well.
      - They articulate a vision.
      - They provide intellectual stimulation.
      - They provide individual consideration.
      - They provide inspirational motivation.
      - They arouse strong emotions and identification with themselves.
      - They transform their followers by teaching them.
   2. They contrast with charismatic leadership in a key element. Charismatic leaders may keep their followers dependent on them.
   3. The Multifactor Leadership Questionnaire (MLQ) is used to measure transformational leadership qualities.
   4. Followers of transformational leaders tend to engage in organizational citizenship behavior.
   5. See Table 13-5. Guidelines for Being a Transformational Leader.

D. **Leading Teams: Special Considerations**
   1. As more and more organizations move to teams, especially self-managed teams, leaders need guidelines for effective management/leadership of these teams.
      - Build trust and inspire teamwork.
      - Expand team capabilities.
      - Create a team identity.
      - Make the most of team differences.
      - Foresee and influence change.
   2. Team leadership is not directive or even participative. One must use a very different style.

IV. <u>Contingency Theories of Leader Effectiveness</u>
    The complexity of leadership leads some to a contingency model, adapting leadership behavior to the immediate situation. The different theories all tie to two things, a) adjusting to the context, and b) a concern for leader effectiveness.

A. **LPC Contingency Theory: Matching Leaders and Tasks**
   1. The theory comes from Fiedler. In the essentials of the theory, there is a recognition that leadership takes place in a context. Success is determined both by the leader's traits and the elements of the situation.
   2. The characteristics of the leader include:
      - "esteem liking" for the least-preferred co-workers (LPC). The key element, it is the leader's tendency to evaluate favorably or unfavorably the person with which it is most difficult to work.
      - the degree of leader's control over 1) his/her relationship with the group, 2) the degree of structure of the task to be performed, and 3) the leader's position power.
   3. Predicted success of the leader.
      - Low LPC (task-oriented) leaders do best in high or low control situations.
      - High LPC (relations-oriented) leaders do best in moderate control situations.
      - See Figure 13-10. LPC Contingency Theory: An Overview.
   4. Research provides moderate support. Results both support and contradict the theory. The theory has been criticized for its ambiguity in classifying situations and for the instrument used to collect data on it.
   5. Application of the theory has proved promising despite the mixed research results. Using the questionnaire, leaders have been matched with what appears to be more appropriate situations with promising results.

B. **Situational Leadership Theory: Adjusting Leadership Style to the Situation**
   1. The theory was developed by Blanchard and Hershey. They concentrate on the maturity of the follower--their willingness to take responsibility--and adjust task and relationship behaviors of the leader accordingly.
   2. The mix of task behavior and relationship behavior lead to four styles.
      - <u>Delegating</u> - when responsibility is largely turned over to followers because they are willing and able.
      - <u>Participating</u> - when followers are able but unwilling to perform, the leader provides high support.
      - <u>Selling</u> - when followers are unable and unwilling to perform, the leader provides both direction and support.
      - <u>Telling</u> - when followers are unable to perform but willing, the leader provides high direction but little support because it's not needed.

Instructor's Notes

3. To choose the appropriate response, leaders must:
   - diagnose the situation.
   - identify the appropriate style.
   - implement an appropriate response based on the style.

You Be the Consultant
1. Students may apply either the LPC or the Situational Leadership model, even though the case best fits the LPC Model.
2. Improving leadership style requires a fuller assessment of the situation. Either provide more detail, or have the students qualify their answers by explaining how they picture the work situation.
3. Students will want to make the President low LPC--focused on relationships--but it may be that he is already low LPC--"nobody listens to me"--and not exerting control. The context the students see is key to their answers, because an argument could be made for either style--depending. Isn't contingency leadership wonderful?

Instructor's Notes

C. **Path-Goal Theory: Leaders as Guides to Valued Goals**
   1. This theory contends that followers will react favorably to the extent they perceive the leader as helping them to attain goals by clarifying paths and rewards.
   2. Leaders can adopt one of four basic styles in accomplishing this task.
      - Instrumental style is directive, provides guidance, and establishes work schedules and rules.
      - Supportive style establishes good relations with subordinates and satisfies subordinates' needs.
      - Participative style has the leader consulting with subordinates and has subordinates participate in decisions.
      - Achievement-oriented style sets challenging goals and seeks improvements in performance.
   3. Which style is best. It depends on:
      - the characteristics of the subordinates.
      - the work environment.
      - See Figure 13-12. Path-Goal Theory: An Overview.

D. **Normative Decision Theory: The Right Time for Employee Participation**
   1. This theory, developed by Vroom and Yetton, focuses on how much participation employees should have in a decision.
   2. Leaders adopt one of five distinct methods for reaching decisions. No one method is preferred, and the success of the method depends on the situation.
      - See Table 13-4. Potential Strategies for Making Decisions.
   3. Selection of the best approach depends on two issues.
      - The quality of the decision, the extent to which it will affect group processes.

- The acceptance of the decision, the degree of commitment among subordinates needed for its implementation.
- See Table 13-5. Decisions Rule in Normative Decision Theory.

4. To determine the impact of these two elements, a leader goes through a decision tree of questions.
   - See Figure 13-13.
5. The model is appealing, because it fully accounts for employee participation and gives leaders clear guidance.
6. Problems include the fact that managers tend to rate their own past decisions as most effective. Also, outsider raters tend to see groups as more effective.

E. **Substitutes For Leadership Theory: When Leaders are Superfluous**
1. Kerr and Jermier propose that other factors may be substituted for a leader's influence.
2. Various factors may:
   - neutralize the effects of leadership, say if people are indifferent to the rewards a leader controls, for example.
   - be substituted for leadership, say if people are highly professional and find their work satisfying.
3. What conditions limit the impact of leadership?
   - Individual characteristics - when subordinates have a high level of knowledge, high level of commitment, or high level of experience.
   - Job structure - jobs are either routine or are very interesting.
   - Characteristics of organizations - work norms, strong feelings of cohesion, and technology affect job performance.
4. Research seems to support this theory.
   - See Figure 13-14. Evidence of the Tendency to Overestimate the Importance of Leadership.
5 Why does everyone think leadership is so important?
   - People have romanticized it.
   - People perceive companies more favorably if their results are attributed to top management than to other factors.
   - Leaders are important in some contexts.

Summary and Review

Questions For Discussion

1. <u>What are the major differences between leaders, dictators, and managers?</u>
    Answer - Fundamentally, it is subordinate participation and willingness to follow leaders decisions. Also, the issue of vision versus carrying out the vision. Students will offer other important insights as well.

2. <u>It has often been said that "great leaders are born, not made." Do you agree? If so why? If not, why?</u>
    Answer - While students' answers will vary, clearly the text takes the position leaders can be made; otherwise, why study the phenomenon and advise people on how to behave, i.e. grid training, etc.? Students who favor a trait or charismatic approach will say they are born. Help students see their perspective on what constitutes leadership affects their answer. Students should see the implication that they all can exercise leadership, given the opportunity and circumstance.

3. <u>Argue for or against the following statement. "The best leaders encourage participation from their subordinates."</u>
    Answer - Students will begin arguing their experience and feelings, which will lean toward a pro position. Help them apply Vroom and Vetton's Normative Decision Theory. Look for their application of the rules and the decision tree. See Table 13-5 and Figure 13-13.

4. <u>In your experience, do most leaders have a small in-group? If so, what are the effects of this clique on other group members?</u>
    Answer - Student answers will vary. It may be helpful to share your own experience, as faculty, you've certainly experienced one side or the other of this question and probably both.

5. <u>Explain how the process of attribution is involved in organizational leadership.</u>
    Answer - How a leader perceives his/her subordinates affects his/her behavior toward them, assignments given, expectations of performance, etc. It also leads to self-fulfilling prophecy as people respond to how they are treated.

6. <u>Consider all the people who have been President of the United States during your lifetime. Which of these (if any) would you describe as charismatic? Which of these (if any) would you describe as transformational? Why?</u>
    Answer - An excellent but difficult question. Students will tend to answer by political orientation or not have a clue because of disinterest. Be prepared to offer examples of behavior of the last four presidents and the apparent consequences of that behavior. Students will tend to be evaluative of the consequences and miss the focus of the question, whether or not this was charismatic or transformational leadership.

7. <u>Concern for people and concern for production are two recurring themes in the study of leadership. Describe the way they manifest themselves in various theories of leadership.</u>
    Answer - LMX, attribution theory, and charismatic leadership focus on people, as it is how they interact that determines leadership effectiveness. Transformational leadership and team leading consider both. Contingency models seek to balance the elements. LPC and Situational focus on people, as it is their interaction or level of maturity that dictates leadership style. Path-Goal and Normative focus on task, what is done and how.

Case in Point: Mary Kay Cosmetics: Where Success is Not Merely Cosmetic.

1. <u>What does Mary Kay Ash do that makes her not only a charismatic but a transformational leader</u>?

   Answer - An interesting question that could be debated, but as for being transformational she clearly: 1) articulates a vision, 2) provides intellectual stimulation, 3) provides individual consideration, 4) inspires motivation, 5) arouses strong emotions and identification with herself, and 6) teaches her followers.

2. <u>What do followers attribute to Mary Kay that makes her so effective as a leader</u>?
   Answer - Her people orientation.

3. <u>What leadership characteristics does Mary Kay exhibit</u>?

   Answer - Self-confidence. Vision. A people orientation. The ability to inspire. Creation of loyalty to herself, etc.

Skills Portfolios
Experiencing Organizational Behavior
Determining Your Leadership Style
1. Photocopy or retype the questionnaire to separate it from the answers.
2. Encourage students to answer <u>how</u> they would do it, not <u>what</u> they think should be done.
3. Consider giving the instrument before the students read the chapter or you lecture on the topic.
4. Before administering, give a short lecture on the fact that leadership style is not personality nor a rating of how good or bad an individual is. Some students see one style as "better as a person" style than another, rather than as behavior tied to a situation.

Scoring
1. Score as directed.
2. Consider tabulating on the board how many you have of each leadership style.
3. The brevity of the questionnaire may result in some students' having fairly close scores in two or more style categories.

Questions for Discussion
1. In discussing Question #2, go back and go through the eight questions and discuss where each style would be most effective. (Drawback--students may see these as the 'right' answers for each question and feel they did badly on the 'test.')
2. Discuss as directed.

Working in Groups
Identifying Great Leaders in All Walks of Life
1. Administer as directed.
2. Consider grouping students by their interests: sports, politics, etc. This will lead to more rapid development of names and more common ground shared in the discussion.

Questions for Discussion
1. Students may need their texts or notes for discussi.
2. Discuss as directed.

Chapter 14 - The Work Environment: Culture and Technology

Learning Objectives

After reading this chapter you, should be able to

1. Define *organizational culture,* and describe the role it plays in organizational functioning.
2. Distinguish between *dominant cultures* and *subcultures* and the various types of organizational cultures that may exist within organizations.
3. Identify various mechanisms by which organizational culture is created.
4. Describe and give examples of various techniques used to transmit organizational culture.
5. Summarize the effects of organizational culture on both organizational and individual performance.
6. Explain why and how organizational culture is likely to change.
7. Identify the four major types of technology identified by Perrow.
8. Define and give examples of *automation,* and explain how people are affected by the use of automation in the organizations within which they work.
9. Describe how *technology* can be used in organizations for purposes of assisting people with disabilities, monitoring job performance, improving the quality of customer service, and improving the environmental quality.

Chapter Contents   Page

Introduction

I. Organizational Culture: Its Basic Nature   469
     A. Organizational Culture: A Definition   470
     B. Culture's Role in Organizations   471
     C. Cultures Within Organizations: One or Many?   471
     D. Types of Organizational Cultures   472

II. The Formation and Maintenance of Organizational Culture   473
     A. How is Organizational Culture Created?   474
     B. Tools for Transmitting Culture   475

III. Organizational Culture: Its Consequences and Capacity to Change   478
     A. The Effects of Organizational Culture   478
     B. Why and How Does Organizational Culture Change?   480

IV. Technology: Its Role in Organizations   483
     A. Classifying Technology's Basic Dimensions   484
     B. Automation in Today's Organizations   486
     C. Human Responses to Automation   488

V. Using Technology in Modern Organizations   490
     A. Assistive Technology: Helping People With Disabilities Work Productively   490
     B. Computerized Performance Monitoring: Management by Remote Control   492
     C. Technological Aids to Customer Service   494
     D. Environmentally Friendly Technology: Design for Disassembly   495

Summary and Review   497
Questions for Discussion   498
Case in Point   498
Skills Portfolio   499
    Experiencing Organizational Behavior   499
    Working in Groups   499

Chapter Outline

Instructor's Notes

Case Preview: An excellent example of how apparent similarities between companies may be superficial and raise a variety of issues when they try to merge. The story ends well, but note, it took over three years for the acceptance by the acquired company of Marks and Spencer to come.

Introduction

1. **Organizational culture** is a collective of the shared beliefs, expectations, and core values of the people in the organization.
2. Organizational culture is a function of internal elements and is shaped by the external environment as well.
3. The chapter :
   - focuses on the interplay of culture and technology.
   - describes the basic nature of organizational culture and its role.
   - describes how organizational culture is formed and maintained.
   - looks at the effects of organizational culture on the individual and the organization's functioning.
   - reviews the role of technology in organizations.
   - examines how people respond to automation.
   - looks at how technology is used to improve employees' work lives and effectiveness.

I. Organizational Culture: Its Basic Nature
   A. **Organizational Culture: A Definition**
      1. It is the cognitive framework of attitudes, values, behavioral norms, and expectations shared by organization members.
      2. There are seven elements used to describe an organization's culture.
         - Innovation.
         - Stability.
         - Orientation toward people.
         - Results-orientation.
         - Easygoingness.
         - Attention to detail.
         - Collaborative orientation.

3. How an organization manages or responds to each of these elements describes its culture.

B. **Culture's Role in Organizations**
    1. An organization's culture plays several important roles.
        *   It provides a sense of identity for members.
        *   It generates commitment to the organization's mission.
        *   It classifies and reinforces standards of behavior.
    2. See Figure 14-2. The Basic Functions of Organizational Culture.

C. **Cultures Within Organizations: One or Many?**
    1. Large organizations often have several cultures within them.
    2. Subcultures form among people with similar attitudes and values along occupational, professional, functional, or geographic lines.
    3. The **dominant culture** is the overarching personality of an organization, its core values.
        *   See Figure 14-3. Values of the Dominant Organizational Culture and Subcultures.

D. **Types of Organizational Culture**
    1. There are four categories of cultures.
        *   <u>Academy</u> - provides opportunities to master many different jobs and to move from one to another.
        *   <u>Club</u> - age and experience are highly valued.
        *   <u>Baseball team</u> - identifies stars who are very talented and highly paid, but who aren't loyal to the organization. Direction is inventiveness.
        *   <u>Fortress</u> - Focus is survival.

II. <u>The Formation and Maintenance of Organizational Culture</u>
    A. **How is Organizational Culture Created?**
        1. There are numerous factors contributing to a company's culture.
            *   Company founders are key in setting the attitudes and values of the company.
            *   The organization's experience with its extended environment creates the niche the company seeks to fill.
            *   Internal interaction forms the shared interpretations of events and actions which shape company action and reaction.
            *   See Figure 14-4. Organizational Culture as Shared Meanings.

2. The practical applications of this are many.
   - Interventions to change attitudes or performance must be tailored to each group within an organization.
   - There needs to be increased contact across functions to reinforce the shared values and beliefs.
   - Small events can carry big messages.

B. **Tools for Transmitting Culture**
   1. <u>Symbols</u> are material objects that connote meanings beyond their intrinsic content. Such as:
      - buildings.
      - decor.
      - slogans.
      - perks (cars, jets, etc.).
   2. <u>Stories</u> illustrate key aspects of an organization's culture and come from formal and informal sources.
   3. <u>Jargon</u> is the special language that defines a culture. It is the everyday language that sets the organization apart.
   4. <u>Ceremonies</u> are celebrations of the corporate values and assumptions.
   5. <u>Statements of principle</u> define the culture in writing by making explicit statements of the ways the company will work, by offering a code of ethics.

III. <u>Organizational Culture: Its Consequences and Capacity to Change</u>
   A. **The Effects of Organizational Culture**
      1. Organizational culture pressures individuals to "go along" to think and act consistently with the existing culture. Culture impacts:
         - <u>organizational performance</u>. There is no compelling evidence that one organizational culture is better than another at influencing for optimum performance.
         - <u>length of employment</u>. See Figure 14-6. Voluntary Survival: Its Connection to Organizational Culture.
         - <u>person-organization fit</u>. How closely individual values and goals match the organization's.

   B. **Why and How Does Organizational Culture Change?**
      1. Changes in external events, markets, technology, government policies, etc., force organizations to change, and hence their cultures to change.
      2. There are three main forces for organizational change.
         - <u>Composition of the workforce</u>. Over time, the people entering an organization change it.
         - <u>Mergers and acquisitions</u>. See Table 14-1. Mergers and Acquisitions: A Potential Source of Culture Clashes.
         - <u>Planned organizational change</u>.

You Be the Consultant
1. Change is inevitable. No organization is fixed, it changes or dies.
2. You may need to refer students back to organizational diversity to gather information on how other cultures might affect the way a business is run.
3. The conflict here will be between the founder's values and the new values brought by new employees. Help students recall that company mission, organizational experience, etc., will provide some stability. Are the changes core value changes or secondary changes?

The Quest for Quality
ServiceMaster Uses Incentives to Create Safety-Conscious Culture
1. The plan to penalize managers' budgets is a significant culture shift for any organization. What external factors brought ServiceMaster to such strong steps?
2. Why would managers resist this change if it would save the company money and ultimately pay them better as a result?
3. What were the practical consequences of this new safety-conscious culture?

Instructor's Notes

IV. Technology: Its Role in Organizations

Technology refers to the physical and mental processes used to transform inputs into usable outputs. It is a means to get things done. Technology is impacting both individual behavior on the job, as well as the functioning of organizations.

A. **Classifying Technology's Basic Dimensions**
　1. Technology is classified by two basic dimensions.
　　• Exceptions - the degree to which an organization makes use of standard inputs to turn out standard outputs.
　　• Problems - the degree to which the situations encountered are either easy to analyze, allowing for programmed decision making, or complex and difficult to analyze, calling for nonprogrammed decisions.
　　• See Table 14-2. Perrow's Matrix of Technologies.
　2. The **matrix of technologies** includes:
　　• routine technology, which uses highly standardized inputs and outcomes.
　　• craft technology, involving standard inputs and outcomes, but more difficult to use to analyze problems.
　　• engineering technology, where there are many exceptions in inputs and outputs.
　　• non-routine technology, faces exceptions with more difficult decisions.

B. **Automation in Today's Organizations**
　1. **High technology** - employs electronic tools. Some examples of high technology are the following.
　　• Advanced manufacturing technology (AMT) - computer-guided process.

- Computer-integrated manufacturing (CIM) - computers control process, gather information.

- Computer-aided design and engineering (CAD/CAE) - computers build and simulate products.
- Industrial robotics (IR) - computer-controlled machines perform complex processes.
- Flexible manufacturing systems - manufacturing processes relying on computer-controlled machines to produce low volumes of products at costs to rival mass-produced ones.

2. **Automation** is the process of using machines to perform tasks otherwise performed by people. It is characterized by:
   - greatly improved efficiency.
   - being very expensive.
   - See Figure 14-8. Manufacturing Technology: Advancing at a Rapid Pace.

The Organization of the Future
Java: "Virtual Software" Coming Soon To a Computer Near You
1. A fascinating case of how technology is changing.
2. How might this affect the way companies buy and update their computer hardware and software?
3. What are the implications for tomorrow's workforce (your students)?

C. **Human Response to Automation**
   1. Technology's impact on people is the main impediment to its advance and widespread use.
      - It impacts **jobs** in that increased efficiency through automation/technology eliminates and redesigns jobs--a fact not lost on labor unions.
      - A shake out of companies not able to invest in the latest technology and therefore unable to complete.
      - **People working with machines** doing more and enjoying their work more as a consequence.
      - Jobs will need to be redesigned and kept interesting in order to keep employees motivated.
      - There will be **new jobs and new challenges** as the work world and the nature of work are radically changed by automation/technology.
      - See Figure 15-9. The Impact of Automation: A Summary.

V. Using Technology in Modern Organizations
   A. **Assistive Technology: Helping People with Disabilities Work Productively**
      1. These are devices and other solutions that help individuals with physical or mental problems perform various actions needed to do their jobs.

- See Table 14-3. Assistive Technology: Some Examples.
2. They create a <u>competitive advantage</u> for the employer by letting them tap qualified but disabled employees.
3. There is a <u>demographic imperative</u>. As the working population ages, they need assistance in performing their jobs.
4. Companies must comply with the *Americans with Disabilities Act* (ADA) by making reasonable accommodation to disabled workers in the performance of their tasks.
5. Companies also have <u>legal requirements</u> they must meet. The intensity of this effort has created a new position in some companies, the <u>Assistive Technology Coordinator</u>.

B. **Computerized Performance Monitoring: Management by Remote Control**
1. Enables managers/supervisors to "look-in" on employees doing their jobs. While popular with companies, it is not always well received by employees. It changes the nature of the superior-subordinate relationship.
2. Arguments in favor of CPM.
    - It gathers objective performance information.
    - It is a valuable source of feedback.
    - It gathers information for planning, training, and work loads.
3. Argument against CPM.
    - it is an invasion of employees' privacy.
    - it creates an atmosphere of distrust.
    - it can be a source of stress.
    - employees dislike it.
    - supervisors dislike the additional workload it entails.
    - See Figure 14-10. Computerized Performance Monitoring: A Mixed Bag of Results.

C. **Technological Aids to Customer Service**
1. After a time of depersonalization of customer service through technology, technology is being used to repersonalize it by:
    - <u>delivering personalized service</u> by keeping track of individual customers' needs and preferences.
    - <u>augmenting service</u> by providing customers with additional support.
    - <u>transforming business</u> by developing entirely new practices to better satisfy customer needs.

<u>Instructor's Notes</u>

D. **Environmentally Friendly Technology: Design for Disassembly**
   1. 94% of materials taken from the earth enter the waste stream within months.
   2. Some countries, such as Germany, have taken aggressive stands through legislation to protect the environment.
   3. **Design for disassembly (DFD)** is the process of designing and building products so that their parts can be reused many times and then safely disposed of.

Summary and Review

Questions For Discussion

1. <u>Characterize the culture of any organization with which you may be familiar by describing the core characteristics collectively valued by its members. Would you consider it an academy, club, baseball team, or fortress?</u>

   Answer - Answers will vary by student. Have students describe each type of culture when they claim it for their organization to ensure they understand the different cultures.

2. <u>You are founding a new company. Describe how you might either intentionally or unintentionally affect its culture. How might your influences linger within the organization long after you have left it?</u>

   Answer - Your personal values and beliefs will affect how you behave, who you recruit and give responsibility to, and how company policies and procedures evolve. Since the employees and the policies will remain after you leave, that will continue to influence the organization.

3. <u>What kinds of events might be responsible for the changing of organizational culture? Explain why these events are likely to be so influential.</u>

   Answer - Students can cite any of the various influences mentioned in the text. Suggest types of organizations when you ask students which influences are likely to be strongest to help them see that their affect may vary by organization.

4. <u>Select a major business close to where you live. Then, using Perrow's system for classifying technology, categorize the types of technology employed by the company.</u>

   Answer - Selection of business will vary by student. See Table 14-2, Perrow's Matrix of Technologies, to assess student's evaluation.

5. <u>It may be said that automation may lead to unemployment on the one hand and new opportunities for employment on the other. Explain this apparent contradiction.</u>

   Answer - The fact that automation reduces the number of workers needed while creating the need for people to service and manage the automation is one way to explain it. Also, the use of automation will unemploy low-skill, relatively uneducated workers while creating high-skill, high-pay jobs for technically competent, educated workers.

6. <u>Describe how technology can be used to improve: a) work opportunities for people with physical handicaps, b) the quality of customer service delivered, and c) the quality of the physical environment.</u>

    Answer - a) It can help people by enhacing remaining skills and abilities or by making it easier to work with the disability. b) Delivering personalized service by keeping track of individual customers' needs and preferences, augmenting service by providing customers with additional support, and transforming business by developing entirely new practices to better satisfy customer needs. c) The use of Design for disassembly (DFD) -the designing and building products so that their parts can be reused many times and then safely disposed of.

7. <u>Do you think the practice of computerized performance monitoring (CPM) is ethical? Why or why not? What benefits and costs may be expected from using CPM?</u>

    Answer - This is a question that will have a variety of answers. Students should understand that all supervisors monitor workers, that's their job. Even with teams, someone monitors performance. CPM is largely an electronic tool. Students will still be uncomfortable with the idea, but a company has the right and the obligation to know what its employees are doing. The question is how much should they monitor.

Case in Point: Putting the "Service" Back into United Parcel Post

1. <u>In what ways has UPS's organizational culture changed? What factors stimulated these changes?</u>

    Answer - The change was largely motivated by external factors, customer dissatisfaction and eroding market share as more aggressive and technologically advanced companies cut in on their customers.

2. <u>What barriers would you suppose UPS faced in changing as it did?</u>

    Answer - It's founders' values, this is the way we've always done it, "if it's not broke, don't fix it," unfamiliarity with new technology, etc.

3. <u>How has UPS used technology to improve its customer service?</u>

    Answer - Students should note package tracking, customized pickup and delivery scheduling, etc.

<u>**Skills Portfolios**</u>
<u>Experiencing Organizational Behavior</u>
What is Your Customer Service Orientation?

1. Many students will think they've not been involved in customer service. Ask how many have worked at McDonald's, the dining halls, etc. Any job where they did things for others, involves customer service. Help them to see it.
2. Ask students to cover the scoring information as they take the questionnaire.

Scoring
1. Score as directed.

Questions for Discussion
1. Discuss as directed.

<u>Working in Groups</u>

Assessing Organizational Culture

1. Consider, with administration permission, administering the questionnaire in some campus department or functional area.
2. The questionnaire will have to be retyped and copied for administration.
3. Brief students on how to conduct themselves. Select students carefully, do not use the entire class as some students simply won't handle this task appropriately, for a variety of reasons.
4. Talk to students about confidentiality. The results of the questionnaire should be keep within the class and not discussed with others. In one case a graduate student's spouse was fired and 'blacklisted' because members of the student's class openly discussed feedback in this type of situation and embarrassed the company owners in their community.

Scoring

1. Score as directed.

Questions for Discussion

1. Discuss as directed, reminding students to also keep the discussion contents within the class.

Chapter 15 - Organizational Structure and Design

Learning Objectives

After reading this chapter you, should be able to

1. Explain the basic characteristics of organizational structure revealed in an organization chart (*hierarchy of authority, division of labor, span of control, line versus staff,* and *decentralization*).
2. Describe different approaches to departmentalization--*functional organizations, product organizations,* and *matrix organization.*
3. Distinguish between *classical* and *neoclassical* approaches to organizational design.
4. Describe how an organization's design is influenced by the environment within which it operates.
5. Distinguish between *mechanistic organizations* and *organic organizations* and describe the conditions under which each in most appropriate.
6. Describe the five organizational forms identified by Mintzberg: *simple structure, machine bureaucracy, professional bureaucracy, divisional structure,* and *adhocracy.*
7. Characterize two forms of intraorganizational design--*conglomerates* and *strategic alliances.*
8. Describe the relationship between organizational design and structure identified in the Woodward studies and the Aston studies.
9. Explain the implications of interdependence on organizational structure.

Chapter Contents

		Page
Introduction		
I.	Organizational Structure: The Basic Dimensions of Organizations	505
	A. Hierarchy of Authority: Up and Down the Organizational Ladder	506
	B. Division of Labor: Carving Up the Jobs Done	507
	C. Span of Control: Breadth of Responsibility	508
	D. Line versus Staff Positions: Decision Makers versus Advisers	510
	E. Decentralization: Delegating Power Downward	510
II.	Departmentalization: Ways of Structuring Organizations	512
	A. Functional Organizations: Departmentalization by Task	512
	B. Product Organizations: Departmentalization by Type of Output	513
	C. Matrix Organizations: Departmentalization by Both Function and Product	515
	D. The Boundaryless Organization: A New Corporate Architecture	517
III.	Organizational Design: Coordinating the Structural Elements of Organizations	519
	A. Classical and Neoclassical Approaches: The Quest for the One Best Design	521
	B. The Contingency Approach: Design According to Environmental Conditions	522
	C. Mintzberg's Framework: Five Organizational Forms	525
IV.	Interorganizational Designs: Going Beyond the Single Organization	528
	A. Conglomerates: Diversified "Megacorporations"	529
	B. Strategic Alliances: Joining Forces for Mutual Benefit	529

V.   <u>Technology: A Major Cause--and Consequence--of Design</u>   532
   A. Technology and Structure in Manufacturing Companies: The Woodward Studies   532
   B. Workflow Integration: The Aston Study   535
   C. Technology and Interdependence: Thompson's Framework   537

<u>Summary and Review</u>   538
<u>Questions for Discussion</u>   539
<u>Case in Point</u>   540
<u>Skills Portfolio</u>   541
   Experiencing Organizational Behavior   541
   Working in Groups   541

Chapter Outline

Instructor's Notes

Case Preview: This case is a classic turnaround story through adaptation to the changing market. It focuses on the changes at Rockwell more through acquisition than internal restructuring. It shows that organizational culture can change, that coordination and cooperation are possible with very positive results.

Introduction

1. **Organizational structure** is the way individuals and groups are arranged with respect to the tasks they perform.
2. **Organizational design** is the process of coordinating these structural elements in the most effective manner.
3. The chapter covers:
   - the place and purpose of the <u>organizational chart</u>.
   - the effective combination of the structural elements of an organization.
   - a discussion of the role of technology as a cause and a consequence of organizational design.
   - the role of environment in organizational design.

I.   <u>Organizational Structure: The Basic Dimensions of Organizations</u>
1. **Organizational structure** refers to the formal configuration between individuals and groups with respect to the allocation of tasks, responsibilities, and authority within organizations.
2. **Organizational chart** represents the connections between various clusters of functions of which an organization is composed in the form of a diagram of the organization's internal structure.
   - See Figure 15-1. The Organizational Chart: A Valuable Guide to Organizational Structure.

A. **Hierarchy of Authority: Up and Down the Organizational Ladder**
1. Hierarchy of authority is the structure of reporting relationships as shown by the organizational chart.
    * Also see, Figure 15-2. Organizational Chart of a Hypothetical Manufacturing Chart.
2. Organizational structure may be tall, with many levels, or it may be flat, with few levels.
3. The trend to "rightsize," or downsize is eliminating many layers in most organizations, based on the assumption that fewer layers reduce waste and enable people to better do their jobs.

B. **Division of Labor: Carving up the Jobs Done**
1. The organizational chart also makes clear how the organization's tasks are divided into specialized jobs.
2. The more tasks are divided into separate jobs, the more specialization an organization has. Larger organizations have more specialization than smaller organizations.
    * See Table 15-1. Division of Labor: A Summary.

C. **Span of Control: Breadth of responsibility**
1. This is the number of people who report to an individual manager, designated by the organizational chart.
    * Wide span of control - responsible for many employees when organizations are flatter.
    * Narrow span of control - responsible for few employees when organizations are taller.
    * See Figure 15-3. Tall versus Flat Organizations: A Comparison.
2. A manager's actual span of control may not be reflected in the organizational chart. He/she may have responsibilities not shown on the chart.
    * Committee assignments.
    * The degree of supervisory control needed.

D. **Live versus Staff Positions: Decision Makers versus Advisers**
1. The division of management responsibility also includes a division of line and staff positions.
    * Line positions have decision-making power.
    * Staff positions provide advice and recommendations.
2. The typical differences between line and staff in responsibilities, commitment, etc., can be a source of conflict.

E. **Decentralization: Delegating Power Downward**
1. In the first half of the century as companies grew, centralization of power was the pattern.
2. The power to make decisions comes in two forms.
    - Decentralization - delegating power to lower levels in organization.
    - Centralization - power retained by a few persons at the top of the organization.
3. Currently there is a growing trend to decentralization for purposes of efficiency, but that is not inherently always the best choice for an organization especially in the case of production-oriented decisions.
    - See Table 15-2. Decentralization: Benefits When Low and When High.

II. Departmentalization: Ways of Structuring Organizations
A. **Functional Organizations: Departmentalization by Task**
1. This is the standard organization by function. It is the most basic approach.
2. Departments or functions are added or deleted as an organization grows or shrinks.
3. Advantages.
    - Sharing of resources.
    - Economies of scale.
    - Avoidance of duplication of effort.
    - Employee specialization.
4. Limitations.
    - Encourages narrow perspectives.
    - Discourages innovation.

B. **Product Organizations: Departmentalization by Type of Output**
1. As organizations grow, they sometimes find a functional structure is not effective. The specialized departments of a functional design may not understand the business of a particular product line or customer.
2. A product organization creates self-contained divisions, each responsible for everything to do with a certain product or product line. Each operates independently.
    - See Figure 15-6. An Example of a Product Organization.
3. Advantages.
    - Focus of energies.
    - Enhances marketing perspective.
4. Limitations.
    - Loss of economies of scale.
    - Attraction and retention of talent.
    - Problems with coordination across product lines.

C. **Matrix Organizations: Departmentalization by Both Function and Product**

1. In response to a U.S. government demand for a specific project manager over any projects done for it, the matrix design evolved.
2. Typically the matrix involves dual authority; two bosses, one functional, the other product.
3. There are three major roles; top leader, matrix bosses, and two boss managers.
4. There are several matrix designs; the temporary overlay, the permanent overlay, and the mature matrix.
5. Organizations adopt matrixes when:
   - they face a complex and uncertain environment and need economies of scale in the use of internal resources.
   - there are several product lines, none of which has adequate resources on its own.
6. Advantages.
   - Permit flexible use of human resources.
   - Enable quick response to changing environment.
   - Enhance communication among mangers.
7. Limitations.
   - Frustration and confusion of having two bosses.
   - One authority system may overwhelm the others if high levels of cooperation required.
   - See Figure 15-7. A Typical Matrix Organization.

D. **The Boundaryless Organization: A New Corporate Architecture**

1. This is simply an organization where the chains of command are eliminated, spans of control are unlimited, and departments give way to empowered teams.
2. Key examples; G.E. and Chrysler small-car engineering group.
3. To work, these organizations must follow the same rules as a successful team. They need high levels of trust and skill.
4. It is often hard for managers to give up this much control, so sometimes political behavior is fostered.
5. There are two types:
   - The **modular organization**, with a central hub of core businesses surrounded by networks of outside specialists that can be added or deleted as necessary.
   - This form is effective for outsourcing of non-core functions. Examples; Nike and Reebok.
   - The **virtual organization** is composed of a continually evolving network of companies linked by shared skills, costs, and access to markets.

<u>Instructor's Notes</u>

> - A partnership is formed to capitalize on these elements and disbanded when objectives are met. Example; Corning. Underlying idea is that each partner contributes its core competencies. It is becoming increasingly popular.
>
> 6. See Figure 15-8. The Boundaryless Organization: Various Forms.

III. <u>Organizational Design: Coordinating the Structural Elements of Organizations</u>

A. **Classical and Neoclassical Approaches: The Quest for the One Best Design**

1. Early theorists, Max Weber, Fredrick Taylor, Henri Fayol, looked for the one best way to organize a company. They believed the most efficient organizations would be highly standardized.
   - Formal hierarchy.
   - Clear rules.
   - Specialization of labor.
   - Highly routine tasks.
   - Highly impersonal atmosphere.
   - This **classical organizational theory** is in disfavor because of its lack of sensitive to human issues.

2. In response to the human issues, spurred by the Hawthorne Studies, improvements in the form of **neoclassical organizational theories** developed.
   - McGregor's Theory X and Theory Y was a reaction to Weber's rigid hierarchy of the bureaucratic form.
   - Argyris argued that managerial domination blocks effective performance and encourages turnover.
   - Likert's System 4 organization opened the door to employee participation in decision making.
   - The neoclassical designs permitted a flattening of organizational structure and broader spans of control, but it still sought the one best way.

B. **The Contingency Approach: Design According to Environmental Conditions**

1. This approach argues that the best design depends on the nature of the environment in which the organization operates. The external environment is connected to the organizational design.

2. The two key elements identified by Burns and Stalker are:
   - Is the company operating in a **stable**, unchanging environment?
   - Is the company operating in an **unstable**, changing environment?

3.   The resulting two approaches are mechanistic versus organic designs.
4.   Mechanistic organizations:
   - are best when the environment is stable.
   - are highly specialized.
   - impose rules.
   - invest authority in a few people.
5.   Organic organizations:
   - are best in a fast-changing environment.
   - require low job specialization.
   - utilize self-control and self-direction of employees.
   - are highly democratic and participative.
6.   The key is matching the organization's structure to its environment. Neither structure is better or worse than the other except relative to its current external environment.
7.   See Table 15-3. Mechanistic versus Organic Designs: A Summary.

C.   **Mintzberg's Framework: Five Organizational Forms**
   1.   The <u>five</u> <u>basic</u> <u>elements</u> (groups of individuals).
      - <u>Operating core</u> - employees who perform basic work of the organization.
      - <u>Strategic apex</u> - top level executives.
      - <u>Middle line</u> - mid-level managers, transmitters of information between the strategic apex and operating core.
      - <u>Technostructure</u> - staff specialists.
      - <u>Support staff</u> - indirect support service providers.
   2.   Result in <u>five</u> <u>specific</u> <u>designs</u>.
      - <u>Simple structure</u> - small, organic, non-specialized, flat structure.
      - <u>Machine bureaucracy</u> - highly specialized, stable, driven by technostructure, centralized authority.
      - <u>Professional bureaucracy</u> - run by operating core, formal, often group/team oriented.
      - <u>Divisional structure</u> - autonomous units coordinated by central headquarters, run by middle managers.
      - <u>Adhocracy</u> - run by support staff, very organic, team oriented.
      - See Table 15-4. Mintzberg's Five Organizational Forms: A Summary.

IV.   <u>Interorganizational Designs: Going Beyond the Single Organization</u>
   A.   **Conglomerates: Diversifies "Megacorporations"**
      1.   This is when an organization diversifies by adding unrelated businesses.

2. Companies do this to:
   - stabilize the business when one industry is down another may be up, equalizing costs/profits.
   - provide built in access to markets and suppliers.

B. **Strategic Alliances: Joining Forces for Mutual Benefit**
   1. Is when two or more companies join their competitive capabilities to operate a specific business.
   2. Alliances come in various forms.
      - Mutual service consortia when two similar companies with similar industries pool their resources to receive a benefit too expensive or difficult to gain otherwise.
      - Value-chain partnership is an alliance of companies in different industries with complementary capabilities.
      - Joint ventures happen when companies come together to fulfill opportunities that require the capabilities of the other company, i.e., a high tech and a marketing company join forces to introduce new technology into the market.
      - See Figure 15-11. Strategic Alliances: A Continuum of Interorganizational Relationships.
   3. Strategic alliances are growing in importance in the global economy. They are formed:
      - to gain entry into foreign markets.
      - to benefit from foreign expertise and capital.
      - for managerial benefits, accessing talent.
      - for improved economies of scale.

The Quest For Quality
The Joint Venture Between Universal Card and TSYS: Lessons Learned
1. A strong example of a joint venture done well.
2. What OB factors contributed to the success of the joint venture?
3. How did each of these companies benefit from the joint venture?

V. Technology: A Major Cause--and Consequence--of Design
   1. The technology selected by a company influences both work processes and future technology choices.

A. **Technology and Structure in Manufacturing Companies: The Woodward Studies**
   1. The best known study on the effects of technology, conducted in the 1960s by Joanne Woodward to discover the relationship between various structural characteristics and organizational performance.
   2. They discovered structures had little to do with success. What they discovered was that it was the fit between structure and the technology used that led to success.

Instructor's Notes

3. They compared three types of technology in use at the time.
   - Small-batch production - custom work, capital equipment not highly capitalized, production of small orders to meet customers' specific needs. Employees were both skilled and unskilled workers depending on their work.
   - Large-batch or mass production - used assembly-line processes and procedures. Employees were both skilled and unskilled workers depending on their work.
   - Continuous process production - the most technologically complex. Production was automated and integrated without a starting or stopping point. Employees were skilled workers.
4. Their results.
   - Different technologies imposed different demands on structure and process.
   - Successful companies were a function of the proper match of structure, mechanistic or organic, with the technology and market served.
   - See Figure 15-13. The Woodward Studies: The Relationship between Technology and Design.
5. Additional studies covering newer technologies have been conducted since, reaffirming the need to match design with technology.
   - See Figure 15-14. Technology and Structure: Evidence of Linkages.

B. **Workflow Integration: The Aston Studies**
   1. These studies sought to determine if Woodward's findings would be repeated in different types of companies.
   2. Their three basic characteristics were:
      - automation of equipment.
      - workflow rigidity.
      - specificity of evaluation.
      - See Table 15-5. Workflow Integration in Different Organizations.
   3. They found that technological complexity was related to structure. In their study, size was a stronger influence than technology.
   4. The argument that there is a **technological imperative**, technology has a compelling influence on structure is an overstatement.
   5. Technology influences smaller organizations more than larger ones.

You Be the Consultant

1. Fabricate-It is a mass production company and might best use a mechanistic structure. Think-It doesn't fit any Woodward category cleanly. Its high tech product and small size puts in between categories for Aston. Students might argue for a small batch structure with an organic structure.
2. What is important here is student analysis of the nature of the companies and their use of technology in their outputs. What rationales are used to justify their choices and categorizations?

Instructor's Notes

C. **Technology and Interdependence: Thompson's Framework**

1. This is the degree to which individuals, departments, or units within an organization depend on each other to accomplish their goals.
2. There are several levels of interdependence.
   - Pooled Interdependence is the lowest level. Units carry out their work independently with little interaction. Rules and procedures are adequate to coordinate work.
   - Sequential interdependence is when one group's output is another's input. The flow is one-way. Meetings and vertical communication are required.
   - Reciprocal interdependence - is when one group's output is other group's input and the flow is two-way. This is true interdependence. Horizontal communication and concerted efforts at coordination are required. See Figure 15-15. Reciprocal Interdependence: An Example.

Summary and Review

Questions For Discussion

1. <u>As organizations grow and become more complex, their designs are likely to change. Describe the various ways in which size may influence organizational design. How are these changes likely to influence individuals?</u>

   Answer - Size will influence the organizational chart, the hierarchy of authority, division of labor, span of control, and how many staff versus line positions the company has. The issue of size should affect the decentralization/centralization of authority, but often does not. It may also affect the structure, such as moving from functional to product to matrix structure. How the changes affect individuals is a broad discussion with a variety of answers ranging from span of control, to participation in decision making, etc.

2. <u>Describe the difficulties you believe will result from implementing a matrix organization.</u>

   Answer - Frustration and confusion of having two bosses. One authority system may overwhelm the others if high levels of cooperation required. See Figure 15-7. A Typical Matrix Organization.

3. Explain various ways in which traditional organizational designs are changing and are expected to change in the future. What problems, if any, do you envision stemming from these trends?

    Answer - This question reviews the entire chapter. Break it down for your students. Problems may be that organizations may have to change back in the future to past structures as the market changes. Some of the modern designs--boundaryless, matrix--may prove ineffective long term. The less structure, the less stability for, and commitment of, employees, etc.

4. What challenges will people face as organizations become increasingly "boundaryless"?

    Answer - It will clearly change employment relationships. It will increase time "between jobs," unemployment for the independent contractors. It will increase competition for small firms. It will make employment by large corporations less appealing.

5. Identify contemporary organizations that are relatively mechanistic or relatively organic in nature. To what extent is each characterized by stable or turbulent environments as predicted by the contingency approach to organizational design?

    Answer - Answers will vary according to students' experience. They will probably pick on auto makers as mechanistic and computer makers as organic. Help them see the changes in auto making--Saturn, Chrysler--and some of the major failures in computer companies-- TI-- that show those stereotypes are not true.

6. Give an example of a specific company you know that fits each of the five organizational forms identified by Mintzberg: *simple structure, machine bureaucracy, professional bureaucracy, divisional structure,* and *adhocracy*. On what grounds does each qualify as an example?

    Answer - Again answers will vary according to student experience. Their descriptions and rationales are key here.

7. Using an example of an organization you know, describe how its prevailing technology is related to its organizational design.

    Answer - Answers will vary. Consider preparing and leading a discussion in how university/college education is changing with 'virtual campus,' non-traditional programs like Nova, etc.

Case in Point: Johnson & Johnson: Separate Companies under One Umbrella

1. What are the advantages and disadvantages of J & J becoming more highly centralized?

    Answer - Advantages--economies of scale, better coordination of efforts, quick tailored responses to the market, etc. Disadvantages--layoff of excess employees, slower decision making, slower response to the market.

2. Is J & J a boundaryless organization? If so, why? If not, how would it have to change to become one?

    Answer - No since a boundaryless organization has eliminated the chains of command, spans of control are unlimited, and departments give way to empowered teams. The recentralization process mitigates against this. It would have to outsource more of its non-core functions and form one of the two basic structures: modular organization with a central hub of core businesses surrounded by networks of outside specialists that can be added or deleted as necessary, or the virtual organization, composed of a continually evolving network of companies linked by shared skills, costs, and access to markets. A partnership is formed to capitalize on these elements and disbanded when objectives are met. See Figure 15-8. The Boundaryless Organization: Various Forms.

Skills Portfolios
Experiencing Organizational Behavior
Which Do You Prefer--Mechanistic or Organic Organization?
1. Administer as directed.
2. Consider photocopying or retyping to separate questionnaire from scoring instructions.
3. Score as directed.

Questions for Discussion
1. Discuss as directed.

Working in Groups
Comparing Organizational Structure and Design
1. Consider assigning this as a short 2-4 page team paper.
2. Without telling the students, type up two forms of instructions--those typical of a mechanistic structure and those typical of an organic structure. Set the exercise up as a competition to keep students from sharing information and discovering they have different directions.

Questions for Discussion
1. Have students answer the questions as part of their team paper.
2. Ask them to address what type of organization design they used in their 'organization' to accomplish this task.
3. If you do not use the team paper idea, discuss questions as directed in the text.

Chapter 16 - Organizational Change and Development

Learning Objectives

After reading this chapter you, should be able to
1. Identify why it is important for organizations to change.
2. Describe the major forces responsible for *organizational change.*
3. Identify the conditions under which organizational change is likely to occur.
4. Explain the major factors making people resistant to organizational change and some ways of overcoming them.
5. Describe the major techniques of *organizational development.*
6. Evaluate the effectiveness of organizational development efforts.
7. Debate the idea that organizational development is inherently unethical.

Chapter Contents   Page

Introduction
I.   Organizational Change: An Ongoing Process   545
     A. Change is a Global Phenomenon   546
     B. The Message is Clear: Change or Disappear   546
     C. The Learning Organization: Benefiting From Change   548

II. Forces Behind Change in Organizations   549
     A. Planned Change   550
     B. Unplanned Change   554

III The Process of Organizational Change: Some Basic Issues   556
     A. Targets of Organizational Change: What Is Changed?   556
     B. Readiness for Change: When Will Organizational Change Occur?   559

IV. Resistance to Change: Will Organizational Change Be Accepted?   560
     A. Individual Barriers to Change   560
     B. Organizational Barriers to Change   561
     C. Overcoming Resistance to Organizational Change: Some Guidelines 562

V.   Organizational Development: The Implementation of Planned Organizational Change   563
     A. Survey Feedback: Inducing Change by Sharing Information   563
     B. Sensitivity Training: Developing Personal Insight   564
     C. Team Building: Creating Effective Work Groups   565
     D. Quality of Work Life: Humanizing the Workplace   567
     E. Management by Objectives: Clarifying Organizational Goals   568

VI. Critical Issues in Organizational Development   569
     A. The Effectiveness of Organizational Development: Does it Really Work?   570
     B. What Should Be the Main Focus of OD: Process or Results?   571
     C. Is Organizational Development Inherently Unethical? A Debate   573

Summary and Review   575
Questions for Discussion   575
Case in Point   576
Skills Portfolio   577
    Experiencing Organizational Behavior   577
    Working in Groups   577

Chapter Outline

Instructor's Notes

Case Preview: DiNicola has changed Zales, radically and the jewelry business along with it. This case shows how organizational development and change can have bottom-line impact and result in financial success. But a question lingers. Is Zales, still Zales? Sales, price cutting, volume, more outlets; do these mean this is a different company or the same company doing business differently?

Introduction

1. The pressure for change is enormous. The question isn't whether or not to change, it is when and how much.
   - See Figure 16-1.
2. Social science methods designed to implement needed organizational change are **organizational development**.
3. The chapter:
   - looks at the process of organizational change and the different forces that act on organizations to bring change.
   - explores major issues involved in the process of organizational change, such as what is changed, when, why people resist, and how to overcome resistance.
   - examines the techniques and critical issues of organizational development.

I. Organizational Change: An Ongoing Process
  A. **Change is a Global Phenomenon**
    1. It is common among international companies.
    2. See Figure 16-2. Organizational Change: An International Phenomenon.

  B. **The Message is Clear: Change or Disappear**
    1. 62% of new ventures fail to last five years.
    2. See Table 16-1. The Ten Oldest Companies in America.

3. There are two levels of changes:
    - **first-order change** is continuous without major shifts in the way an organization operates.
    - **second-order change** is more complex, involving major shifts on many different levels of the organization.

C. The Learning Organization: Benefiting From Change

1. An organization that is successful is successful at acquiring, cultivating, and applying knowledge that can be used to help it adapt to changes.
2. This kind of organization follows four basic steps.
    - Knowledge acquisition - the process of tapping the expertise of its employees to create a pool of knowledge from which to draw.
    - Information distribution - both the distribution and understanding of information.
    - Information interpretation - accurate interpretation.
    - Organizational memorization - how information is stored to be tapped when needed to initiate change.
3. Most organizations do not take these steps.

II. Forces Behind Change in Organizations

A. Planned Change

1. Changes in products or services.
2. Changes in organizational size and structure.
    - Restructuring.
    - Downsizing.
    - See Table 16-2. Alternatives to Layoffs.
3. Changes in administrative systems. Changing policies, reward structures, etc.
    - Dual-core model - describes the phenomenon that changes in the administration of an organization tend to come from top management--top-down, while changes in the central work of the organization tend to come from the technical side of the organization--bottom-up.
4. Introduction of new technologies.
    - Desktop computers.
    - Computer-automated technology.
    - Robotics.
    - See Figure 16-4. Technology: A Key to Quality.
5. Advances in Information Processing and Information.
    - Satellite transmission systems.
    - Fiber-optics.

- Fax machine and portable telephones.
- Teleconferencing.

The Ethics Angle

No Layoffs: A Hallmark of Life at Hallmark

1. This story provides an excellent opportunity to debate both the ethics and reality of layoffs. Help students think about the specific reasons a company lays off employees.
2. As students consider this mini-case, ask them, "Who are the stakeholders in a layoff situation?" This might help them see the broad effects of a layoff.

The Quest for Quality

Competitive Intelligence: Planning Change by Learning about the Competition

1. Students may want to debate the ethicality of competitive intelligence. Ask any marketing students (who clearly would use it) to argue against it and any OB/HRM students argue for it (who would clearly be against it) to help them see each other's side.
2. Stress that this process uses legal means and public information and is actually a part of TQM, benchmarking.
3. Discuss its importance with students and what alternatives they would have if they chose to not use competitive intelligence.

Instructor's Notes

B. **Unplanned Change**
   1. Changing employee demographics.
   2. Government regulation - often in response to a problem.
   3. Economic competition.
   4. Performance gaps between actual and expected levels of performance.

III. The Process of Organizational Change: Some Basic Issues
   A. **Targets of Organizational Change: What is Changed?**
      1. There are three primary areas of change for an organization.
      2. Changes in the organizational structure.
         - Power structure.
         - Span of control.
         - Basis for departmentalization.
         - Classifying policies and procedures.
      3. Changes in technology.
      4. Changes in people using a three-step process.
         - Unfreezing - getting people ready for change.
         - Changing - making the change.
         - Refreezing - institutionalizing, making the change permanent.
         - See Figure 16-7. Changing People: Some Basic Steps.

Instructor's Notes

B. **Readiness for Change: When Will Organizational Change Occur?**
   1. People are ready to change when three factors are present.
      - When employees are dissatisfied with current conditions.
      - When a desirable alternative is available.
      - When there is a plan for achieving that alternative.
   2. See Figure 16-8. Organizational Change: When Will it Occur?

IV. Resistance to Change: Will Organizational Change Be Accepted?
   A. **Individual Barriers to Change**
      1. Economic insecurity.
      2. Fear of the unknown.
      3. Threats to social relationships.
      4. Habit.
      5. Failure to recognize need for change.
      6. Demographic background.

   B. **Organizational Barriers to Change**
      1. Structural inertia.
      2. Work group inertia.
      3. Threats to existing balance of power.
      4. Previously unsuccessful change efforts.
      5. Composition of the board of directors.

   C. **Overcoming Resistance to Organizational Change: Some Guidelines**
      1. Shape political dynamics.
      2. Educate the work force.
      3. Involve employees in change efforts.
      4. Reward constructive behaviors.

V. Organizational Development: The Implementation of Planned Organizational Change
   A. **Survey Feedback: Inducing Change by Sharing Information**
      1. See Figure 16-9. Survey Feedback: An Overview.
      2. Survey feedback follows three steps.
         - Data collection.
         - Feedback, reporting the information.
         - Analyzing the problems and developing action plans.

B. **Sensitivity Training: Developing Personal Insight**
   1. Comes from the 1940s encounter groups and T-groups.
   2. Places employees in situations where they can feel safe to communicate openly and honestly.
   3. Sessions are wide open as to topics for discussion.
   4. Effectiveness is difficult to assess.

C. **Team Building: Creating Effective Work Groups**
   1. The effort is to get members of a work group to diagnose how they work together and then improve that process.
   2. The process entails several steps.
      - Recognition of problem.
      - Diagnosis of group's strengths and weakness.
      - Developing desired goals for change.
      - Developing action plan to make changes.
      - Implementation of plan.
      - Evaluation of plan.
      - See Figure 16-10. Team Building: Its Basic Form.
   3. Team building requires the participation of all team members.
   4. It is <u>not</u> a one time exercise but a process.
   5. Techniques for team building vary from the basic form in Figure 16-10 to adventure experiences in Figure 16-11.

D. **Quality of Work Life: Humanizing the Workplace**
   1. This involves the creation of a work environment that enhances employee motivation, satisfaction, and commitment.
   2. Techniques discussed earlier in the text to redesign jobs are an essential part of this process.
      - Job enlargement.
      - Job enrichment.
      - Job characteristics model.
   3. Quality circles are small voluntary groups of employees who meet weekly to identify and solve problems.
   4. QWL has a number of benefits to it.
      - Increased job satisfaction.
      - Increased productivity.
      - Increased organizational effectiveness.

5. Two potential pitfalls sometimes hinder achievement of these benefits.
- Lack of labor/management cooperation.
- Plans must be fully implemented.

E. **Management by Objectives: Clarifying Organizational Goals**
1. The process has three steps.
- Mutual setting of goals and development of action plan.
- Implementation and monitoring of progress.
- Evaluation.
- See Figure 16-12. Management by Objective: Developing Organizations through Goal Setting.
2. MBO is designed to get the individual and organization to work together, but management must wholeheartedly support it because of the long-term effort involved.
3. It is one of the most widely used techniques for affecting organizational change.

You Be the Consultant
1. Students can chose from a variety of team building techniques. Help them concentrate on the basic model before they send employees for an adventure trip. Fiscal reality is always important.
2. If students try to solve the problem with quality circles or QWL, bring them back to the problem--team functioning, or lack of it.
3   See Figure 16-10 for the steps of the Basic Team Building Process.

VI. Critical Issues in Organizational Development
A. **The Effectiveness of Organizational Development: Does it Really Work?**
1. There is research that supports the effectiveness of these techniques, but it leads only to a qualified yes, it works.
2. Some studies show quality circles reduce costs and improve employee attitudes, other research shows no benefit.
3. The same is true with sensitivity training.
4. A summary study by Porras and Robertson showed that the major effect of OD interventions was for organizational effectiveness, not individual effectiveness.
- See Figure 16-13. Organizational Development: How Effective Is It?

5. Qualifications of the various findings.
    - OD interventions work better with blue-collar than white-collar employees.
    - Benefits are enhanced by using multiple rather than single techniques.
    - Effectiveness depends on support from top-management.
6. It is clear that it is difficult to assess change.

B. **What Should Be the Main Focus of OD: Process or Results?**
    1. By process we mean how to get things done, by results we mean what should be accomplished.
    2. By definition OD is results oriented.
    3. U.S. management has tended to be the victims of neat packages with great promises attached.
    4. The solution, according to Schaffer and Thompson-- clear goals with a short-term focus.
    5. OD is longer-term focused.

Globalization and Diversity in Today's Organizations

Is OD Universally Effective? Cultural Barriers to Effective OD Interventions

1. This case provides an excellent opportunity for students to integrate their learning from various sections of the book. Have them review chapter 2 for discussion of the case.
2. The case shows simply that OD must, like almost all business practices, be adapted to the culture of the country. What issues does this raise for diversity in U.S. organizations and OD interventions?

C. **Is Organizational Development Inherently Unethical? A Debate**
    1. The debate focuses around several issues.
        - Consideration of individual values when changing organizational values.
        - Focus on the organization and not the individual.
        - Potential for coercion and manipulation.
        - Unequal power relationships.
    2. Such arguments tend to be seen as arguing that management is inherently unethical, since most of what OD does is management practice related.
    3. OD is not inherently unethical or evil. Practitioners make occasional mistakes or may be unethical, but the tool is not the problem.
        - See Figure 16-14. The Ethics of OD.

Summary and Review

Questions For Discussion

1. Some changes in organizations are unplanned, whereas others are the result of deliberate, planned actions. Give examples of each of these varieties of change and explain their implications for organizational functioning.

   Answer - <u>Planned Change</u>. 1. Changes in products or services. 2. Changes in organizational size and structure. 3. Changes in administrative systems. Changing policies, reward structures, etc. 4. Introduction of new technologies. 5. Advances in information processing and information. <u>Unplanned Change</u>. 1. Changing employee demographics. 2. Government regulation--often in response to a problem. 3. Economic competition. 4. Performance gaps between actual and expected levels of performance.

2. Suppose you are having difficulty managing a small group of subordinates who work in an office 1,000 miles away from your home base. What kinds of changes in structure, technology, and people can be implemented to supervise these distant employees more closely?

   Answer - Students answers will vary. Most clearly, the use of technology is essential, be it: video-conferencing, e-mail, computer networks, etc.

3. Under what conditions will people be most willing to make changes in organizations? Explain your answer and give an example.

   Answer - People are ready to change when three factors are present. 1) When employees are dissatisfied with current conditions. 2) When a desirable alternative is available. 3) When there is a plan for achieving that alternative. See Figure 16-8. Organizational Change: When Will it Occur?

4. Suppose that you are a top executive of a large organization about to undertake an ambitious restructuring involving massive changes in job responsibilities for most employees. Explain why people might be resistant to such changes and what steps could be taken to overcome this resistance.

   Answer - There are individual barriers to change. 1. Economic insecurity. 2. Fear of the unknown. 3. Threats to social relationships. 4. Habit. 5. Failure to recognize need for change. 6. Demographic background. There are organizational barriers to change. 1. Structural inertia. 2. Work group inertia. 3. Threats to existing balance of power. 4. Previously unsuccessful change efforts. 5. Composition of the board of directors. Resistance can be overcome several ways. 1. Shape political dynamics. 2. Educate the work force. 3. Involve employees in change efforts. 4. Reward constructive behaviors.

5. Overall, how effective is organizational development in improving organizational functioning? With respect to what factors does it work or not work?

   Answer - There is research that supports the effectiveness of these techniques, but it leads only to a qualified yes, it works. Some studies show quality circles reduce costs and improve employee attitudes, other research shows no benefit. The same is true with sensitivity training. A summary study by Porras and Robertson showed that the major effect of OD interventions was for organizational effectiveness, not individual effectiveness. See Figure 16-13. Organizational Development: How Effective Is It? It does seem that OD interventions work better with blue-collar than white-collar employees, that benefits are enhanced by using multiple rather than single techniques, and that effectiveness depends on support from top-management.

6. Argue for or against the following statement: "Organizational development is inherently unethical and should not be used."

   Answer - Students can argue either side. Reality is OD that is here to stay. Some key points to look for: 1) Consideration of individual values when changing organizational values. 2) Focus on the organization and not the individual. 3) Potential for coercion and manipulation of employees. 4) Unequal power relationships. OD is not inherently unethical or evil. Practitioners make occasional mistakes or may be unethical, but the tool is not the problem. See Figure 16-14. The Ethics of OD.

Case in Point: Starting Over Is a Shoe-In for Joan and David

1. Describe the planned and unplanned forces responsible for change at Joan & David.

   Answer - Planned change for themselves initially then unplanned change when there was change in the market.

2. What might the Halperns do to help ensure their company's future as a key player in the fashion industry?

   Answer - Answers will vary by student.

3. What factors are likely to make employees of Joan & David resistant to change? How might these be overcome?

   Answer - There are individual barriers to change. 1. Economic insecurity. 2. Fear of the unknown. 3. Failure to recognize need for change. Resistance can be overcome several ways. 1. Educate the work force. 2. Involve employees in change efforts. 3. Reward constructive behaviors.

Skills Portfolios
Experiencing Organizational Behavior
Are You Prepared for Downsizing
1. Administer as directed.

Questions for Discussion
1. Discuss as directed.
2. Encourage students to keep a copy of this questionnaire and to review the questions annually when they are working in their careers.

<u>Working in Groups</u>
Recognizing Impediments to Change--and How to Overcome Them
1. Administer as directed.

Questions for Discussion
1. Discuss as directed.
2. Groups will probably have a great deal of similarity in the barriers, but there will be some differences. Focus on the differences to help the students see how different groups working with the same information can have very different perspectives and understandings of a situation.
3. Students should see that different situations raise different issues. Try to tie in contingency management theory here and show why adapting the context is important to effectiveness.

Part I Video Case—When Employees Become Owners

Video: "The Changing Face of Labor"

Source: *David Brinkley*, September 4, 1994

Summary of Video Content:

This video can be used in conjunction with either chapter 1 "The Nature and Study of Organizations" or chapter 2 "Work in the 21st Century." The original air date of this segment coincided with Labor Day, 1994. Interviewees include employees and executives at Caterpillar, United Airlines (UAL) Chairman and CEO Gerald Greenwald, and Secretary of Labor Robert Reich. The written case focuses on employee ownership at UAL, a topic that also was the cover story in the March 18, 1996 issue of *Business Week*. Greenwald discusses prospects for improved employee productivity and cutting costs to enhance competitiveness.

Suggested Discussions Questions:

1. The video dates to the fall of 1994. A good lead-off question in 1996 or 1997 is, "How well is United doing today?" Ask students what they know about the airline business in general and UAL in particular.

One indicator success is that UAL's stock price has more than doubled since the buyout, in part due to lower costs. Productivity as measured by revenue per employee is increasing, employee grievances are declining, and United is winning market share from American and Delta. (United has been less successful winning market share battles with low-cost carriers such as Southwest). The lesson here is the behavior changes that take place when employees start to think like owners. Still, as noted in the case, United's 20,000 flight attendants did not participate in the buyout because they were unhappy about the pay cuts.

2. Do you think United employees will maintain their upbeat attitudes and cooperative spirits over the long term?

There are internal and external factors to consider. Much depends on Gerald Greenwald's style, in particular his willingness to share power. As he told *Business Week*, "I took the view that we're no longer a company that operates by command and control." If Greenwald leaves and a new chief executive is hired, relations between management and employee-owners could deteriorate. Also, the ESOP coincided with an upturn in demand for air travel that boosted overall industry profits to a record $2 billion in 1995, compared with billions in losses for the five previous years. If the next downturn necessitates fare cuts, the inevitable cost-cutting efforts that ensue will undoubtedly put strains on employee morale.

Part II Video Case—Working Fathers Balance Careers and Families

Video: "The Joys and Risks of the 'Daddy Track'"

Source: *Nightline*, August 14, 1991

Summary of Video Content:

This video ties in well with both chapter 3 "Perception and Learning: Understanding and Adapting to the Work Environment," and chapter 4, "Individual Differences: Personalities and Abilities." Male interviewees include a former Microsoft employee, a Washington attorney, and a representative from the world's largest executive recruiting firm; the female interviewee works for the DuPont Corporation. The first part of the video should be particularly interesting since it involves Microsoft, a company that should be familiar to all class members.

After the class has viewed the video, ask students to comment on the statements made by Microsoft's Gwen Weld. The resulting discussion can then lead directly to the first discussion question.

Suggested Discussion Questions:

1. What role does perception play in the issues raised by the video?

Perception plays an important role, both internally (between employees), and between employees and customers/clients. Jeff Coulter, the former Microsoft employee, notes that coworkers' perception of time may have influenced opinions against him. As he points out, he came in early, when few people noticed, but if he left at 5:00 pm or 5:30 pm, plenty of people saw him leave. Although executive recruiter Lester Korn notes that Les Sotsky, an attorney with Arnold & Porter, Washington's largest law firm, works for a progressive firm where flexibility is possible, Sotsky replies that client perceptions have generally been supportive. Sotsky notes, "[Clients] recognize the struggle that all parents are engaged in." Sotsky also believes that, if others in his law firm are stigmatizing him for taking time off, they haven't expressed it to him.

2. Faith Wohl, the DuPont manager, believes one of the barriers to more family-friendly organizations is middle managers' fears of losing control. Lester Korn, the recruiter, is emphatic that the real issue is that top management can't accomodate the needs of those who want to be on the "Mommy track" or the "Daddy track," for the simple reason that there is great pressure to get the job done. "Work is not a trolley," he says. "You can't get on your career and off your career and on your career. You simply have to stay there and work." Who do you agree with?

This question should spark some good discussion. Students should recognize that, in fact, the situation is likely to vary from company to company. The fundamental issue is striking a balance between the needs of the corporation and the needs of the family.

Part III Video Case—Looking for More Cal Ripkens

Video: *""The Streak: Cal Ripken, Jr."*

Source: *Nightline*, September 6, 1995.

Summary of Video Content:

This video relates to several themes developed in chapters 5 and 6. Cal Ripken, Jr., baseball's "iron man," is the embodiment of the motivated employee, the topic of chapter 5. Ripken's positive attitude towards work and his feelings about his job reflect issues covered in chapter 6. The subject of Cal Ripken is certain to generate a high level of interest among students who follow sports. In addition to Ripken, however, both the video and written case focus on other men and women in ordinary jobs—a waitress and a cook at Baltimore's Hauser's restaurant, for example—who have compiled equally impressive "streaks."

Suggested Discussion Questions:

1. Some might argue that extrinsic motivation—specifically, a $30 million, five-year contract—is the most important factor in Cal Ripken's achievement. If so, why do ordinary employees who earn ordinary wages also compile impressive streaks?

Sports-minded students will probably point out that Ripken's streak has less to do with his superstar salary than with his love of the game of baseball (something that most students can relate to). That can lead to a discussion of "ordinary" employees who love their "ordinary" jobs. Challenge students to ask themselves what kind of jobs or career paths would trigger similar loyalty, enthusiasm, and commitment in them. Remind them that, as pointed out in Chapter 7, the pressures and stress in today's workplace are being compounded by downsizing, reengineering, and other organizational processes.

2. Coach Benny Edens told *The New York Times*, "Basically, I think our society has come to a point where if there's a discomfort, we give in to it. If there's a headache, we stay home rather than work through it. If we have something we'd rather do—stay in the mountains one more day —it's 'I'll take a day of sick leave. You know, I've got 10 coming.' I think today's generation puts themselves in from of their responsibility." Ask students whether they agree with Coach Eden's assessment of younger workers.

To directly connect the discussion with the students' lives, ask for a show of hands of those who have cut class for a "non-emergency" reason (e.g. taking a three-day weekend to visit a friend in another city or taking an extra day to get back from spring break. (Several hands are likely to go up, perhaps with some prodding from the instructor). Ask if students can give a rationale for being "no-shows." Now ask for "war stories" from students who made an extra effort to show up for class or work despite inclement weather, illness, or some other reason.

Part IV Video Case—Do Communication Rituals Hold Back Women in the Workplace?

Video : "He Says She Says —Women's Business Style Is a Handicap"
Source: 20/20, October 21, 1994.

Summary of Video Content: This video profiles author Deborah Tannen, who believes differences in speaking styles between men and women can be detrimental to the way women are perceived in the workplace. The video fits well with all four chapters in Part IV, particularly chapter 9, "Interpersonal Communication." Specifically, Tannen believes that women may be passed over for promotions because of their tendency to be more polite than men. According to Tannen, women say "Thank you," too much, and as a result they unintentionally put themselves in a "one-down" position, while a supervisor or boss is in a "one-up" position. Similarly, brief apologies by women are another ritual that can be interpreted as "it must be her fault." Tannen traces the origin of these rituals to games children play; girls tend to talk while playing, while boys talk less and compete more. Girls share more, negotiate, and are less direct; boys are more direct. Tannen does not claim that one style is better or worse than the other, only that a particular style can more be effective in a given situation.

Suggested Discussion Questions:

1. Can you give some examples of conversational rituals between men and women based on your own experience? In your opinion, are those differences based strictly on gender?

Answers need not focus on the workplace. Student answers will vary depending on their experience. For example: A female colleague will "go drinking" with male friends, but "go out for a drink" with female friends. In the case of "drinking with the guys," the communcation is activity focused, which "going out for a drink with the girls" suggests that drinking is merely a pretext for spending time together in conversation.

2. Do you agree with Tannen's advice that men should offer more praise to subordinates (a female ritual), while women could benefit from the male ritual whereby verbal sparring is not taken personally?

Suggested Follow-Up Assignment: Many organizational experts believe the workplace in the 1990s puts increased pressure on employees to adapt to change. Collaboration, participative leadership, and team building—activities for which women's communications styles seem well suited—will be required for success. Based on your own library research, can you find any evidence that women are, in fact, breaking the glass ceiling in the 1990s? Can any individual successes be attributed to communication style? Finally, is there evidence that men are being forced to alter their communication rituals to conform with organizational trends?

Part V Video Case—Ben & Jerry's: A New Leader to Manage Growth

Video: "Sharing Sweet Success"

Source: 20/20, May 22, 1992

Summary of Video Content: This video, which ties in directly with chapter 13, "Leadership," and with chapter 14 , "Empowering People," features an interview with Ben Cohen and Jerry Greenfield, founders of Ben & Jerry's Homemade Inc. The segment profiles their environmentally-conscious company where senior managers receive salaries only seven times more than the wages that the lowest-paid employees receive. The video serves as a background for the issue raised in the written case, namely Cohen and Greenfield's decision to bring in an executive with more operational and marketing expertise. Although not noted in the case, Holland is the first African-American to be recruited as CEO of a majority-owned franchise business.

Suggested Discussion Questions:

1. Is Ben & Jerry's the type of company you would like to work for? Why or why not?

Cohen and Greenfield embody a distinct type of caring leadership that many students will find attractive. The company's three-part mission statement articulates a vision for doing business that is very much in touch with concerns and interests of students in the 1990s. The "culture of fun" at Ben & Jerry's is also likely to be viewed favorably. (A similar subject is covered in the video on Southwest Airlines.) A key question is whether the corporate culture will change with the arrival of the new CEO.

2. Cohen and Greenfield changed their compensation rules in order to hire their new CEO, Robert Holland, Jr. Do you think the new CEO will change the "flavor" of Ben and Jerry's unique way of doing business?

The issue of executive compensation is certainly timely in the late 1990s. Ask students whether they think Holland's $250,000 salary is reasonable given the challenges he faces. Some students will point out that, notwithstanding Cohen and Greenfield's 7-to-1 policy, salaries are generally set by the marketplace. If Holland can successfully introduce the new line of sorbets and guide the company's entry into international markets, then he will more than justify his salary.

Suggested Follow-Up Assignment: Industry observers note that changes in product-labeling laws may draw consumer attention to the high fat content of Ben & Jerry's ice cream and, ultimately, hurt sales. Jerry Cohen recently appeared on *Oprah Winfrey* to introduce the sorbets, which include such flavors as sweet potato pie. Go to the library and find out whether the new line is being well-received by consumers.

Part VI Video Case—Telecommuting

Video: "Telecommuting" (length: 5:20)

Source: *Business World*, February 3, 1991

Summary of Video Content:

This video is keyed to the Part VI "Organizational Processes." The explosive popularity of cellular telephones, fax machines, computer modems, the Internet, and e-mail messaging ties in directly with chapter 15 "The Work Environment: Culture and Technology." Several issues from chapters 16 and 17 including organizational design, change, and development, also relate to the technology-driven telecommuting revolution. One driving force behind the telecommuting trend is environmental: from earthquakes in California to blizzards in New England, companies are realizing the importance of incorporating telecommuting into crisis and disaster planning.

Suggested Discussion Questions:

1. Summarize the advantages and disadvantages of telecommuting.

Advantages include better employee productivity, improved customer satisfaction, and quicker market responses. Telecommuting employees report lower stress levels resulting from a less hectic pace and increased job satisfaction because they are better able to manage their work and personal lives. Another advantage is environmental: Telecommuters use less gas, which results in less pollution. Organizations in Houston, Philadelphia, Chicago, and seven other metropolitan areas are currently looking for ways to comply with EPA rules that took effect in the fall of 1994. The EPA set targets for cutting air pollution from auto emissions by 15 percent. A program of employer-trip reduction that includes telecommuting is one tool in the war against pollution. Although not mentioned in the case, Disadvantages echo some of those highlighted in the Part II video case about working fathers, namely fewer advancement possibilities and reduced career momentum.

2. Why are some managers and supervisors reluctant to support telecommuting? How can that reluctance be overcome?

As noted in the written case, managers ask, "How can I tell if someone is working when I can't see them?" Telecommuting requires managers and supervisors to be more trusting, and to realize that, instead of equating attendance with output, they must measure results irrespective of where those results are achieved. This can be challenging. One way to increase acceptance is to standardize procedures, policies, and guidelines for telecommuting so that everyone can agree on the "groundrules."

Video Guide: Southwest Airlines

Video: Southwest Airlines

Source: *Business World,* March 15, 1992

Summary of Video Content: This video profiles Herb Kelleher, the iconoclastic chief executive of Southwest Airlines. While the video can be used in conjunction with several chapters, it meshes particularly well with chapter 4 "Individual Differences," chapter 9 "Interpersonal Communication," and chapter 13, "Leadership." Herb, as he is known throughout the company, has been described by *Fortune* magazine as the "High Priest of Ha-Ha." Kelleher has created an organizational environment in which employees are encouraged to be themselves and have fun in the process. Elizabeth Pedruck Sartain, vice president of the People Department at Southwest, says, "We feel this fun atmosphere builds a strong sense of community. It also counterbalances the stress of hard work and competition."

In 1994, Southwest received the Department of Transportation's "Triple Crown" award for best one-time performance, best baggage handling, and fewest customer complaints. Southwest recently turned back competitive challenges by United Airlines in the key California market. To contribute to such outstanding results, employees must view themselves as team members who are willing to pitch in on any job. Rita V. Bailey, Southwest's manager of corporate employment, says, "We just want the kind of person who can relate to everybody and everything."

Suggested Discussion Questions:

1. Southwest celebrated its 25th anniversary in 1996. What challenges does the company face as it looks ahead to its next quarter-century?

Perhaps the most obvious issue is succession: Kelleher, a chain smoker, will soon be 70 years old. Inevitably, someone will have to take his place. Yet, much like Sam Walton at Wal-Mart, many observers consider the charismatic leader inseparable from the success of the corporation. The key question is: Will Kelleher's successor be able to sustain the culture of fun that has been a key ingredient in the company's success? Another issue concerns growth: As Southwest expands beyond its regional routes, it may be difficult to maintain the same high level of productivity that has helped it achieve its status as the industry cost leader.

2. Southwest receives more than 100,000 job applications in a given year. Why do so many people want to work for the company? What type of person would be most likely to succeed there?

The corporate culture is a clear lure for many people. The company looks for common sense, a sense of community based on values, and self determination. As Kelleher says, "We look for attitudes. We'll train you on whatever you need to do, but the one thing we can't do is change inherent attitudes in people," he says.

Video Guide: Hiring Practices at Japanese-Owned Companies

Video: "No Room at the Top" (length 16:47)

Source: *20/20, September 27, 1991*

Summary of Video Content:

This video, like the Part II video on worker fathers, touches on a lawsuit filed by an employee who sued a company for terminating his employment. In this instance, the employer was a Japanese company with operations in the United States, and the plaintiff was an American. The video ties in well with chapter 1, "The Nature and Study of Organizations," and chapter 2, "Work in the 21st Century." The issues raised in the video also relate to the four chapters in Part IV, "Group Processes." Although the video first aired in 1991, it is still timely in light of the allegations of harassment that surfaced in 1996 at a Mitsubishi assembly plant in Illinois. Another current issue that relates to the case involves actions by American companies such as AIG to lay off employees and hire foreign workers for up to five years as allowed by the Immigration Act of 1990 signed by President Bush.

The central issue in this video is whether Japanese executives prefer to promote Japanese rather than American employees. Chet Mackentire, who is profiled in the video, handled optical computer disk sales for the File Products Division (FPD) of the Ricoh Corporation. He sued his former employer for discrimination under Title VII of the Civil Rights Act of 1964. Ricoh's position was that Mackentire was laid off for business reasons, not because he was Caucasian and American. One expert interviewed in the video, a California headhunter, downplays the discrimination issue, claiming that differences in culture, values and leadership style are the reasons Americans are sometimes passed over for promotion at American subsidiaries of Japanese companies.

Suggested In-Class Activity

After the class has viewed the video, ask for a show of hands by students who believe that Mackentire has a strong case. Then, ask students to predict the outcome of the lawsuit. After some discussion, instructors can provide the following details: Mackentire's original case was dismissed by summary judgment in the United States District Court for the Northern District of California. The court "found there was no evidence to support Mackentire's theory that the layoff was discriminatory, and that there was substantial evidence that it was due to business necessity." Mackentire's attorney submitted an appeal to the Ninth Circuit Court of Appeals on May 25, 1993; on June 2, 1993, the circuit judges upheld the lower court's summary judgment. In the discussion, the judges wrote, "Ricoh offered affidavits stating that FPD was losing money, running into the millions of dollars annually. It also offered evidence that it reorganized the division to de-emphasize the product for which Mackentire was most responsible."

Video Guide: Workplace Violence

Video: "Back with a Vengeance" (length 14:14)

Source: *20/20*, April 16, 1993

Summary of Video Content: This video examines the killing of bosses and co-workers by disgruntled former employees who seek revenge after they have been fired or laid off. The video can be shown in conjunction with Chapter 7, "Career Development and Work Stress," and Chapter 11, "Helping, Cooperation, and Conflict in Organizations." The issue of workplace violence in America has been gathering momentum for a decade after a spate of five post office killings introduced the phrase "going postal" into the management lexicon. A recent study by the Justice Department indicates that as many as 1 million employees are subjected to on-the-job violence annually. (It should be noted, however, that homocide by co-workers, former employees, customers or clients accounts for only 9 percent of workplace homocides.) Catherine Crier examines incidents of employee violence at Fireman's Fund Insurance Company, in Tampa, Florida, and the Convair Division of General Dynamics in San Diego, California. Although one expert notes that it is hard to determine who will be violent, the profile generally points to middle-aged white males with a history of frustration and blaming others for their problems. However, that profile fits thousands of employees, so experts advise that companies pay attention to the firing process. However, two particular problems are noted in the video. First, in corporate America, it is hard to use strange behavior on the part of an employee as a basis for firing. Second, corporations are ill equipped to handle employees who come back in a violent manner. At the end of the video, Arnold Castro, a union shop steward at General Dynamics, advises that attitudes shown by company management must "become more humanistic."

Suggested Discussion Questions:

1. Why is workplace violence likely to continue to be an issue in the 21st century?

The downsizing trend is likely to contribute to violence. As workforces are being slashed, the employees who remain are burdened with a heavier workload. Notes psychologist Charles Labig, "People at all levels of the company are feeling anxiety. That stress can easily flow into blaming and being angry at executives."

2. What should companies do about violence?

One expert notes that most companies are dealing in a reactive, after-the-fact manner than in a proactive manner aimed at violence prevention. Cambridge, Massachusetts-based Polaroid has well-developed policies in place. Managers are trained to recognize signs indicating when a worker might become violent and to look for signs of domestic abuse. The company also offers paid leaves for emotional distress.

Video Guide: Controversy Over Sensitivity Training by the FAA

Video: "When the Tables are Turned" (length 7:45)

Source: 20/20, September 16, 1994

Summary of Video Content:

Bob Brown reports on a controversial sensitivity training program that the Federal Aviation Agency (FAA) provided for air traffic controllers in Chicago. The video ties in directly with chapter 17, "Managing Organizational Change and Development," as well as chapter 7, "Career Development and Work Stress." The video is also timely in light of the allegations of harassment that surfaced in 1996 at a Mitsubishi assembly plant in Illinois. During the late 1980s and early 1990s, the FAA received complaints from women and minorities that, when they reported to work, they were walked gauntlet between male co-workers who made suggestive comments or engaged in inappropriate touching. After determining that many of the male air traffic controllers didn't think twice about such incidents or considered them to be "all in fun," the FAA hired an outside firm to assist FAA employees in conducting three-day training sessions. During one component of the workshop, women sat on two rows of chairs while men were forced to "walk a gauntlet" between them. Air controller Douglas Hartman participated in one of the workshops, and subsequently filed a lawsuit against the DOT, alleging he was forced to walk the gauntlet against his will and that the women grabbed him in a no-holds-barred fashion. Hartman was suing on the grounds that elements of the training bordered on the types of sensitivity it was supposed to prevent. As Hartman told an interviewer, "Don't use abuse to fix abuse." However, other participants in the workshop with Hartman disputed his account of what happened, saying there was no gauntlet. In fact, some participants noted that the training was effective and that office conditions improved as a result. As one minority participant asked, "How can [white males] complain about a few minutes of discomfort?" In the end, the FAA stopped using the company that had presented the controversial seminars.

Suggested Discussion Question:

1. Do you agree with Douglas Hartman that it is inappropriate to "use abuse to fix abuse"?

Student response may vary along gender lines. Women students may agree with the view expressed in the video that it's a small thing for men to experience briefly the kind of discomfort to which women and minorities are frequently subjected. Instructors should encourage discussion participation by students who have taken courses in related areas such as gender role development or the psychology of men and women.

PRENTICE HALL, Upper Saddle River, New Jersey 07458

http://www.prenhall.com

ISBN 0-13-568213-4

9 780135 682135